Disability and World Language Learning

Disability and World Language Learning

Inclusive Teaching for Diverse Learners

Sally S. Scott and Wade A. Edwards

ROWMAN & LITTLEFIELD
Lanham • Boulder • New York • London

Published by Rowman & Littlefield
An imprint of The Rowman & Littlefield Publishing Group, Inc.
4501 Forbes Boulevard, Suite 200, Lanham, Maryland 20706
www.rowman.com

6 Tinworth Street, London SE11 5AL, United Kingdom

Copyright © 2019 by Sally S. Scott and Wade A. Edwards

All rights reserved. No part of this book may be reproduced in any form or by any electronic or mechanical means, including information storage and retrieval systems, without written permission from the publisher, except by a reviewer who may quote passages in a review.

British Library Cataloguing in Publication Information Available

Library of Congress Cataloging-in-Publication Data Available

ISBN 978-1-4758-3704-9 (cloth)
ISBN 978-1-4758-3705-6 (pbk.)
ISBN 978-1-4758-3706-3 (electronic)

Contents

List of Tables and Textboxes	vii
Foreword	ix
Preface	xi
Acknowledgments	xv
Introduction	xvii
1 Disability, Student Diversity, and Inclusive Teaching	1
2 Setting the Stage for an Inclusive Language Learning Classroom	19
3 In the Classroom	45
4 Assessment of Student Learning	69
5 Getting Started	91
6 Conclusions	107
References	115
Index	117
About the Authors	121

List of Tables and Textboxes

TABLES

An Educational Journey	6
The Principles of Universal Design for Instruction Applied to World Language Learning	13
Sample Grading Rubric for an Oral Activity	82
Sample Rubric for Final Grades That Incorporates Student Choice	83

TEXTBOXES

Syllabus Examples	31
Student Responses to the Prompt, *For me learning a foreign language is like...*	38
Strategies for Supporting Use of the Target Language	49
Guiding Questions for Making Homework Assignments More Inclusive	64
Class Participation Self-Assessment Rubric	88
Self-Check: Inclusive Classroom Features Before Class Begins	96
During the First Three Weeks: Using Inclusive Strategies to Connect with Students	102

Foreword

We who teach world languages are at a crossroads and must answer the "what's the value" question with more assurance and evidence than ever before. College and university administrators, state legislatures, and large swaths of the American public are asking openly whether certain learners and certain programs are too costly for the fiscal health of our educational institutions. The challenges are acute for languages other than English and for students with disabilities whose learning styles are perceived to be outside of the presumably affordable norm. Shortsighted cost-benefit analyses do not inspire. English only? Disability as liability? As foundational concepts for strategic planning, their impact is profound and profoundly limiting.

    Wade Edwards and Sally Scott enlarge the scope of this calculus with deep understanding of our profession and our students. They champion world language study as a bedrock value of higher education, presume competence of students with disabilities, and locate barriers to learning within pedagogy itself. This rich collaboration between a professor and a professional in disability services has culminated in a book that can enable us to ready our disabled students—and all of our students—to take the languages they have learned into the world beyond college. Eloquent, persuasive, and eminently practical, *Disability and World Language Learning: Inclusive Teaching for Diverse Learners* is the book that teachers need right now.

    I encourage readers to think broadly about what they will find within these pages. Students with disabilities are at its center *as learners*, and disability respected, cast not as a fundamental deficit but as a fact of life. These students are rightfully regarded as full participants in language courses, in majors, and in studies abroad. Access has moved from the realm of service provision toward an everyday ethic of removing barriers, a genuine and positive transformation of the classroom itself. Questions for reflection enable teachers to evaluate their practices and take their next steps in designing accessible, effective instruction. Comprehensive and logical assessment tools are among the ample resources that teachers can and should apply immediately.

Every step of the *how* is firmly grounded in the *why*. Edwards and Scott show us that we, who elevate the intellectual promises of language study and proffer career opportunities and friendships across linguistic borders as lifelong learning outcomes, can realize these outcomes for disabled students, too. They do so, remarkably, while emphasizing pleasure in teaching at every turn. More than a milestone, *Disability and World Language Learning* lays the pathway itself, putting a sure foundation under our highest aspirations.

Dr. Elizabeth C. Hamilton
Associate Professor of German
Associate Dean, College of Arts and Sciences
Oberlin College

Preface

THE CONTEXT AND NEED FOR THIS BOOK

As a professor of French and an administrator of a campus disability resource office, we form in some respects an unlikely partnership. A department chair and scholar in French literature is often ensconced in teaching, research, and the work of Academic Affairs on campus. A director of disability resources is typically involved with the work of the Student Affairs division to promote campus inclusion and compliance with federal laws. But our conversations about language learning and students with disabilities revealed some common ground and mutual professional interests. Some of our early conversations revolved around questions and topics that may be familiar to you:

- I received a letter from the disability resource office saying a student in my class is eligible for extended test time. Can you tell me about the student's disability, so I can help her more?
- A student approached me after class and said he has an Individualized Education Program (IEP) from high school that he needs to continue. What's an IEP and does that apply in college?
- An incoming student has contacted me to say she had a waiver for foreign-language course work in high school. She has a foreign-language learning disability and will not be able to complete the college's language requirement.

It was around this last topic—the question of whether there exists a learning disability specific to world language learning—that we began our extensive work in the area of language learning and disabilities. Our campus had a procedure in place to address changes to any of the general education requirements, including the language learning requirement. But in recent years, the number of students seeking waivers or course substitutions for the language requirement had been growing. We were curious. Why was this the case? Were incoming students less qualified than those in the past? Were more students experiencing disabilities? Had something changed at the high school level that was affecting student expectations for accommodations and support in college? Was there something to this notion of a "disability" in language learning?

As we examined this issue, we found little support for the notion of a learning disability specific to second-language acquisition. Research over several decades in the area of learning disabilities (LD) has found that students who had difficulty in their native language with the fundamental tasks of reading, writing, speaking, and listening often have a reemergence of difficulty when learning a second language. Students with a diagnosis of dyslexia, a form of learning disability, are characterized by difficulty with encoding and decoding language—the very building blocks of reading and writing that are the focus of beginning language learning. But LD come in many forms, and each student profile is unique in terms of the impact and severity of the disability.

At the college level, students with LD are often very bright and have developed strong compensation strategies for completing college-level work. An assumption of language learning aptitude based on disability label would be misguided. Research has failed to identify a "profile" or "disability" focused solely on second-language acquisition. But logically, those students who had trouble mastering their native language may need additional support when learning a second language. For some, this difficulty is extreme, and a substitution of required coursework may be warranted, but for most students, it is a matter of appropriate instruction, support, and time.

As we explored the demands on students with LD in the world language classroom, we became more aware of other students who may encounter barriers to learning related to a disability. For example, consider the student with an attention deficit disorder who has difficulty with auditory working memory. The frequent learning experience of listening to a question and responding in the target language may be very challenging. Consider a student with autism whose language use or prosody is somewhat atypical in the native language. Pitch, loudness, tempo, and tone of speech in a world language classroom may make small group work and interaction with peers difficult. A student with a chronic health disability such as cancer, sickle cell anemia, or chronic fatigue syndrome may encounter barriers to class attendance that limit essential opportunities for practice and interaction in the target language.

As we discussed these many student learning profiles, we kept coming back to the question of instruction. If we examined our teaching, were there ways to make the classroom more inclusive of these learners? If we could incorporate inclusive strategies, would that reduce the number of students who need to request a waiver or course substitution of the language requirement?

When we began our collaboration, the concept of Universal Design for Instruction (UDI) was just emerging in the field of postsecondary disability. In contrast to existing approaches to disability access that emphasize legal compliance and retrofitted "special" accommodations for individual students, UDI focuses on designing instruction and assessment for a broad range of diverse learners.

This resonated strongly with both of us for several reasons. It was a natural match for our mutual value of equitable teaching and the recognition that every student needs the opportunity to learn additional languages in today's world. UDI also embodies a new way to view disability as a predictable aspect of student diversity. The burgeoning academic field of disability studies refers to this as a social model of disability. For readers who are interested in the theory behind this approach, we will provide more context on disability models in chapter 1.

We have now spent over a decade exploring this topic and working with faculty on inclusive language learning. Local and federal grants through the U.S. Department of Education have supported our work to better understand the barriers to learning that exist for students with disabilities. We have collaborated with colleagues and trained national and international audiences of faculty to identify key aspects of planning and delivering instruction that is inclusive of students with disabilities. We look forward to sharing these strategies with you in the pages that follow.

Acknowledgments

After "hello" and "goodbye," the first expression encountered in the world language classroom is typically "thank-you." A sign of respect and openness, the ability to express gratitude is a critical skill for any learner encountering a new language and culture for the first time. It reminds us that language learning is never solitary, that the path to proficiency is populated with neighbors, friends, and guides.

Writing about language learning similarly relies on the support of a host of friends and professional partners. If we learn to speak a new language in order to hear what others have to say, we, the authors, would like to say "thank-you" to all those students, teachers, and colleagues who shared their stories with us as we were researching and writing this book.

Our appreciation, first, is to the leadership and development team of Project LINC (Learning in Inclusive Classrooms), the federally funded grant project in which many of the strategies included in this book were conceived and refined. Lily Anne Goetz, Geoff Orth, and John Reynolds were the seasoned professors at Longwood University who helped us make initial connections with language learning and Universal Design for Instruction. Maggie Butler in the Office of Disability Resources also provided insights and resources that kept us on track.

Longwood colleagues Sue Hildebrandt, Kate Neff, and Heather Mueller Edwards helped flesh out first concepts and wrote early modules on inclusive instruction.

Instructors in Longwood's modern languages program—some brand-new colleagues, some long-serving veterans; all hardworking and talented educators—were willing and valuable participants in year-long workshops that helped us enhance pedagogical strategies for newer learners.

Several Longwood students participated in focus groups and official interviews that allowed us to understand potential barriers and aids to language learning for students with disabilities and other diverse learners. In addition, more than 500 anonymous beginning- and intermediate-level students gave us feedback about instructional strategies.

To these partners, to our editor Tom Koerner, and to all who have shared their expertise, experience, and enthusiasm over the course of the past decade, we are truly grateful.

Sally S. Scott
sally@ahead.org
Midlothian, Virginia

Wade A. Edwards
edwardswa@longwood.edu
Farmville, Virginia

Introduction

HOW TO USE THIS BOOK

This book is written for language instructors. While the focus of the content is on college-level learning, many high school language teachers will find this book useful as well. The diversity of students and the kinds of learning barriers that are described are present in secondary and postsecondary classrooms alike, and the application of the Universal Design for Instruction (UDI) principles benefits students in both settings.

The chapters are organized to follow a progression of ideas that parallel classroom planning. Beginning with an understanding of why each topic is important, chapters then move through the process of planning for student diversity, interacting with students in the classroom, and assessing student learning in inclusive ways.

Each chapter provides a brief overview of important content areas, followed by questions that prompt you to start applying concepts to your own teaching. Case studies and questions allow you to go deeper in your thinking about inclusive teaching, and the UDI resolutions provided for each case model the process of using UDI to enhance your teaching.

In chapter 1, "Disability, Student Diversity, and Inclusive Teaching," the focus is on increasing awareness and understanding of the diverse students in your classes with a particular focus on diverse students with disabilities. This chapter also introduces the important framework of UDI that serves as a foundation for the inclusive teaching strategies in this book.

Chapter 2, "Setting the Stage for an Inclusive Language Learning Classroom," looks at strategies for planning instruction to be welcoming and inclusive from the first day of class. The focus on anticipating student diversity and integrating inclusive features covers physical, informational, and attitudinal aspects of course planning.

Chapter 3, "In the Classroom," turns to the topic of instructional strategies. Selecting teaching techniques and being intentional in all interactions with students are the focus of this chapter. We discuss ways to make key instructional strategies such as use of the target language, group activities, and homework more inclusive of students with disabilities and a variety of learners.

Chapter 4, "Assessment of Student Learning," reexamines the familiar topic of assessment from a UDI perspective. Core assessment and feedback strategies including error correction and grading rubrics are discussed with strategies for maintaining academic standards while promoting inclusive and equitable approaches for all learners. Student self-assessment is highlighted as a useful way to support student metacognition.

Chapter 5, "Getting Started," discusses concrete ways to continue the process of becoming an inclusive language instructor. Campus resources and connections are described as important sources of continued growth in your awareness of student diversity on your campus. We also provide a number of suggestions for getting started in the classroom, ranging from quick changes that can be made tomorrow to developing a long-term plan for modifying your instruction over multiple semesters.

Chapter 6 provides the conclusion with a review of some remaining questions we often encounter in our workshops. We also challenge you to start to consider how you can share what you have learned about UDI and inclusive teaching with your colleagues in the world language department and across campus.

Student examples, quotations, and case studies are used throughout the book. They are based on the authors' research and many years of experience in the classroom. We encourage you to explore the questions for reflection and the UDI resolutions on your own for quick strategies and insights that are immediately practical for your teaching. For those with the luxury of exploring teaching with colleagues, whether in graduate teaching-assistant training, departmental professional development, or workshops with the campus teaching and learning center, the case studies and content of this book will provide for thought-provoking discussion.

Chapter 1

Disability, Student Diversity, and Inclusive Teaching

When educators talk about teaching, they often focus on the actions of the teacher. How will the course be structured? What textbook or curricula should be used? How can the classroom provide a rich sensory experience with visuals, music, and interaction? At the core of these important planning questions is the basic assumption that an essential goal of teaching is to provide a learning environment that is student centered.

But who are today's students? The diversity of students reflected in college classrooms is more prevalent and varied than ever. This chapter describes national trends and changing forms of diversity, including the predictable presence of students with disabilities in your classroom. It also connects new ways of thinking about disability with standards for foreign-language education that emphasize the importance of inclusive teaching. The discussion concludes with an overview of Universal Design for Instruction (UDI) and the guiding principles that are used throughout this book to stretch and bolster your growing awareness and use of instructional strategies that are inclusive of students with disabilities.

GROWING STUDENT DIVERSITY

Let's begin, as many language classes do, with stereotypes.

Although Peter Weir's 1989 film *Dead Poets Society* recounts the story of an old-fashioned New England boarding school in the 1950s, it conjures up a familiar perception of the American college experience that lingers still today. The students at the fictional Welton Academy—wealthy, young, white, and male—live, study, and play on an elegant residential campus, preparing to pursue careers that mirror those of their socially connected fathers. Motivated by poetry, live theater, and school dances, the students make their upscale academy the center of their lives.

Popular portrayals of college life have, of course, broadened since the 1950s to reflect a more realistic picture of the typical student experience. Despite the enduring strength of the stereotype, most American college students are not preppy New Englanders.

Jane Smiley's 1995 novel *Moo*, for instance, populated by female protagonists and set at a Midwestern land-grant university, reminds us that elite liberal arts institutions occupy but one corner of the vast American postsecondary neighborhood. Richard Russo's *Straight Man* (1997) and Tom Wolfe's *I Am Charlotte Simmons* (2004) further remind us that the American university is truly multivalent and that the students who attend postsecondary institutions are anything but homogenous.

Awareness of this campus diversity has become a key component in the development of classroom instructors. Using data from the U.S. Census Bureau, Hainline, Gaines, Long Feather, Padilla, and Terry at the Association of American Colleges and Universities (AAC&U) reported in 2010 that fully half of the U.S. population is comprised of individuals currently called "minorities." The percentage of white non-Hispanic students is projected to decrease in the next decade from 64% to 59%, while there will be increases in the proportion of total enrollments for blacks (13.0–14.5%), Hispanics (11.6–13.8%), Asian/Pacific Islanders (6.7–7.6%), and Native Americans (1.0–1.2%).

In 2014, the National Center for Education Statistics noted that, for the first time, the total percentage of students from these minority groups combined is larger than the percentages of whites in public-school classrooms nationwide. In individual states with large minority populations, such as California, Texas, and Hawaii, these figures are unsurprising. In 2014, for instance, the University of California system—the state's flagship institution with nine different campuses—admitted more Latino students (29%) than white students (27%) (Williams, 2014). In the future, the shift in national demographics will undoubtedly continue to change the makeup of college campuses even outside areas where ethnic diversity is a relatively new phenomenon.

Most college students today are women, who make up 57% of all higher education enrollments. This is a sweeping change when compared to the 1970s, when about 40% of undergraduates were women. By 2020, that figure is projected to climb still higher to 61.5%. The gap between women and men is even more pronounced within minority cohorts. For instance, just 37% of black undergraduates are male.

In addition to changes in the racial, ethnic, and gender composition of the college student population, the AAC&U notes that college students are projected to be somewhat older than those currently considered "traditional aged." While population projections show a 9% increase in the matriculation of students aged 18 to 24, the cohort of students between 25 and 29 years is expected to increase by 25% over the next decade.

The economic background of the average college student is also changing. Lower-income students continue to make up an increasing percentage of the undergraduate population even though, since 1994, the cost of college tuition has risen faster than both inflation and the consumer price index. In 1971, Harvard University's $2,600 tuition amounted to about 13 weeks' worth of the median household's annual income of $10,285. Today, the median household needs to work for almost a year to pay the full price.

The increased percentage of students from lower economic backgrounds unquestionably changes the typical student experience. On the one hand, a larger percentage of students now work while they take classes. Already by 2007, roughly 46% of full-time and 81% of part-time college students were employed. So many part-time students currently work that professionals now distinguish students-who-work from workers-who-study (Gaston et al., 2010).

On the other hand, students from lower-income levels may also demonstrate lower levels of college readiness. Their path to a four-year college degree often starts at a community college, particularly if they represent a minority community. Overall, then, trends point to a typical student who is less prepared than those of previous generations but who must also juggle academic responsibilities with part-time or full-time employment.

In short, we are a long way from Welton Academy. Today's typical students differ wildly. The young, white, male, and privileged group of *Dead Poets Society* is more the exception than the rule. In addition to variations in ethnic backgrounds or socioeconomic status, contemporary students may be transfer students, war veterans, homeless, or food insecure. They may also have a disability.

Reflection

Pause for a minute and think about these national trends in college student diversity.

- Do any of these data surprise you?
- How is this diversity different than when you were a student?
- What forms of diversity have you observed among the students you teach?
- How might this diversity influence your interaction in the classroom?

STUDENTS WITH DISABILITIES

According to the National Council on Disability, the proportion of college undergraduates with disabilities has increased from approximately 6% in

1995 to 11% of all college students in 2012. This figure means that about two million undergraduates currently report a diagnosed disability. Disability itself, however, is far from a homogenous descriptor of student characteristics and identity.

At the college level, disability is defined by the Americans with Disabilities Act (ADA). Enacted in 1990, this federal law frames disability as a significant impairment to a *major life activity*. Major life activities are functions that are important in most people's daily lives, including seeing, hearing, eating, sleeping, walking, standing, lifting, bending, speaking, breathing, learning, reading, concentrating, thinking, communicating, and working (Skomsvold, 2014).

On college campuses, this categorization encompasses students with conditions that vary as widely as celiac disease (an immune disorder restricting the consumption of gluten) to a learning disability that impacts reading comprehension to bipolar disorder (a mental health condition involving extreme mood swings that impact energy and ability to think clearly).

While national data vary somewhat, the National Center for Educational Statistics (Skomsvold, 2014) reported that the four most frequent types of disabilities disclosed by college students include

- learning disabilities (LD) (31%),
- attention deficit hyperactivity disorder (ADHD) (18%),
- psychiatric/mental health disorders (15%), and
- chronic health conditions (11%).

It is notable that the majority of these students have what is frequently described as non-apparent disabilities. Wheelchair users, by contrast, comprise only 7% of college students with disclosed disabilities, while students with perceptible sensory disabilities such as deaf/hard of hearing and low vision or blindness are present in much fewer numbers, reflecting 4% and 3%, respectively.

As with other forms of student diversity, the makeup of the disability population changes and shifts over time, often reflecting evolving educational practices, policy implementation, or broader societal changes. For example, federal laws mandating special education services for students with disabilities in elementary and secondary education were established in 1975. By the 1990s, colleges consequently experienced a surge of incoming students with LD. With earlier diagnosis and individualized special education services under this new law, many more students were now preparing and becoming qualified for college-level study.

Between 2000 and 2010 colleges saw an increasing presence of students with ADHD and mental health concerns due to increased public awareness and diagnosis. Most recently colleges have seen growth in the number of students on the autism spectrum. In the 1990s the Centers for Disease Control began observing an upward trend of children with this diagnosis. Current national data show between 1% and 2% of college students with disabilities disclose that they are on the autism spectrum.

With the broad definition of disability that applies in higher education, it is not surprising that there is a wide variety of disabilities reflected in the college student population. Not all students will have disabilities that you can see or perceive. Not all students will have disabilities that impact learning in your classroom. But these characteristics are nonetheless present and contribute to the diversity of today's college student population.

However, it is important to remember that no single aspect of student identity exists in isolation. Being mindful of intersectionality, or the ways that different social identities overlap, consider these 2012 data from the National Center for Education Statistics:

- Fifty-seven percent of college students with disabilities are female, a figure very similar to peers without disclosed disabilities.
- Students with disabilities more frequently reported their race as black (18% vs. 16%) or two or more races (4% vs. 3%) than nondisabled peers.
- Over one-third (36%) of students with disabilities were aged 30 or older compared to 24% of the nondisabled college population.
- Seven percent of students with disabilities indicated they were veterans in contrast to only 3% of the general college student population.

Students with disabilities are now attending postsecondary education at rates similar to students without disclosed disabilities, but their completion rates are much lower; only 34% finish a four-year degree in eight years. According to the National Center for Learning Disabilities, just a quarter of students who received special education services for their learning disabilities in high school chose to disclose their disability and seek assistance in college (Krupnick, 2014).

The National Council on Disabilities reports that while 87% of students with learning disabilities had academic accommodations and supports in K-12, only 19% requested accommodations at the college level. The reasons for this disparity are manifold, though much may be attributed to the impact of the 1975 Education for All Handicapped Children Act. Through updates and amendments, this law is now called the Individuals with Disabilities Education Act (IDEA) (2004). It provides structure and special education funding for students with disabilities only through completion of high school.

Significant changes in services occur as students with disabilities transition to college (see table 1.1). At the K-12 level, special education services and support under the IDEA are mandatory, regulated, and free to the student. Instructors are formally licensed and are responsible for adapting materials

Table 1.1. An Educational Journey

K-12 Experience for Students with Disabilities Mandatory and Free			
Teacher Responsibilities			**Student Responsibilities**
Classroom Experience	Course Materials	Student Support	
—Formally trained in teaching —Adapts materials to students' learning style —Helps student learn and process information	—Always checks students' work —Reminds students of incomplete work —Reviews assignments and due dates	—Structures time for students —Initiates help sessions —Available for talks before and after class —Provides support to parents —Teacher advocates for students	—Attend classes —Begin to learn self-advocacy skills
University Experience for Students with Disabilities Voluntary and Expensive			
Possible Teacher Characteristics and Behaviors	**Student Responsibilities**		
	Classroom Experience	Course Materials	Student Support
—An expert in her or his subject but not necessarily a skilled teacher —Accessible for help during his or her office hours —May expect student to ask for help —May not see all assignments if he or she has a teaching assistant or grader —May not provide reminders of due dates	—Needs to think about and integrate multiple topics —Takes responsibility for absorbing classroom materials —Students' decisions have consequences	—Gets course materials from syllabus —Often gets homework assignments from syllabus —Pays attention to due dates as written in the syllabus —Manages own time —Needs to take notes to be successful	—Student is expected to ask for help sessions —Attends professor's office hours as needed —Should provide parent with any appropriate information —Advocates for self

Source: Used with permission of Student Accessibility Services, University of Vermont (2010).

and providing instruction that meets the student's Individualized Education Program (IEP). They also initiate help sessions, provide support to parents, advocate for the student, and remind students of work as it is due.

At the postsecondary level, where disability concerns fall under the ADA rather than under IDEA, support and services are initiated by the student rather than by the institution. Students may choose to disclose a disability to the school or not. Instructors at this level may expect the student to ask for classroom accommodations while the Federal Education Rights and Privacy Act regulations may prevent communication with parents altogether. IEPs developed in K-12 do not carry over to the postsecondary environment, where responsibility for managing the disability shifts from the institution to the individual student.

While many college instructors are unaware of this significant shift in the life of a student with disabilities, many students themselves are not prepared for this changing role in attaining services. Given the option to disclose a disability or not, entering college freshmen may see this development as a welcome opportunity to shed the disability label. With no special education teacher, no IEP, and no parental sign-off on services at the college level, the student must now monitor his or her own need for accommodations or supports.

Alternatively, some college students may have newly acquired disabilities, such as a traumatic brain injury from a car accident or a newly diagnosed mental illness. These students may be unaware that the disability affects their learning or that support may be needed or even possible.

What does this mean for your classroom? Perhaps you have asked yourself in the past, *Why didn't this student come to me sooner? Why did she wait so long to disclose her disability and request accommodations?* Understanding that students are new to this responsibility of disclosing a disability and requesting services is important context for you as an instructor.

STUDENTS SAY

Aubrianna on disclosing a disability: "The instructor went out of her way to ask about that [the faculty notification letter] which I really liked. It made me less uncomfortable requesting accommodations."

Source: Scott, Hildebrandt, & Edwards (2010)

It may also be tempting to think, *Maybe the student should try my class without these supports. I think she'll be fine.* It is a much more productive relationship to establish a learning environment where the student is aware of potential campus supports and is comfortable talking with you about his or her learning needs in your class. In the following chapters, we provide strategies for making your classroom a welcoming environment for these conversations.

Reflection

Think for a minute about students with acknowledged or unacknowledged disabilities in your classroom.

- What are the challenges you face in providing a learning experience that is inclusive of students with disabilities?
- At a time when higher education is increasingly aware of the importance and value of student diversity, what are the opportunities that students with disabilities bring to your class?

THINKING ABOUT DISABILITY IN NEW WAYS

Diverse college students experience college in diverse ways, a truism that calls for updated learning theories and pedagogical strategies on the part of instructors. The shift from a traditional, medicalized understanding of disability to a more contemporary social model is one such strategy.

In the classroom, a medical model of disability encourages an instructor to address an individual with disabilities on a case-by-case basis, as an exception to the norm. Instructors who subscribe to this understanding of disability might initially consider ways to modify a particular lesson or course to accommodate an unexpected student in the class. Examples of retrofitted accommodations include the addition of specialized seating or the creation of classroom materials unique to the student with disabilities.

While modifying the classroom space or course content can help provide access to various students, modifications are always afterthoughts; they are changes to a program or course or space that initially excluded a student with disabilities.

The complement to the medical model of disability is the social model of disability—a philosophy of approach that distinguishes impairment (something that is individual and private) from disability (something that is structural and public).

The social model of disability recognizes that unavoidable physical impairment is often compounded by needless social exclusion when the educational environment neglects to consider the full range of student diversity. Adherents to a social model of disability recognize that the diversification of American postsecondary institutions represents an opportunity for thoughtful, inclusive curricular design.

In the area of language learning, the American Council on the Teaching of Foreign Languages (ACTFL) has long celebrated diversity in the classroom. Aware that most young language learners are not destined for institutions like the fictitious Welton Academy, ACTFL encourages educators not only to understand the variety of life experiences of the students they teach but also to incorporate that variety into their lesson planning.

World-Readiness Standards for Learning Languages, a collaboration among ACTFL and other professional organizations devoted to foreign-language instruction, presents a vision of what American students should know and be able to do in a second language. Commonly called the ACTFL Standards or the 5 Cs, these principles identify the primary sociolinguistic and cultural elements of language learning and suggest ways to lead students toward a more advanced linguistic and cultural proficiency. *Knowing how, when, and why to say what to whom* is common shorthand for the student skills the standards address.

Initially developed for the K-12 student, the standards have been augmented by individual language task forces to encompass the postsecondary learner. The five interconnected standards are not performance standards but rather content goals. They do not describe how well students are doing, nor do they privilege particular pedagogical methods. Instead, they provide direction and an organizing sense of purpose to instructors. The standards are the following:

- Communication: Students are able to communicate in languages other than English.
- Cultures: Students gain knowledge and understanding of other cultures.
- Connections: Students connect with other disciplines and acquire information.
- Comparisons: Students develop insight into the nature of language and culture.
- Communities: Students participate in multilingual communities at home and around the world.

The most recent edition of the *Standards* has been expanded to include language-specific learning scenarios and sample classroom activities, drafted by active practitioners, that model the outcomes and values of the standards within a target language. These activities are included not to endorse a precise path toward language proficiency but rather as a way to help instructors imagine classroom activities that will advance a student's language skills.

Consider one model activity suggested for college-level French students, a group project on newscasts. The description of the learning scenario is followed by a reflection devoted to the specific standards that the illustration targets. As you read this activity, begin to ask yourself whether there may be barriers present for students with disabilities.

Les Actualités: A French Newscast (postsecondary)

Students in a college intermediate French class prepare and film their own news broadcast, *Les Actualités*. First, they view televised news broadcasts from France or Quebec and compare and contrast American and French or Canadian news broadcasts. As preparation for their own project, students are assigned to play roles and/or participate in the preparation of various segments of the program, for example, news anchor, sportscaster, weather person, traffic reporter, film critic, restaurant reviewer, celebrity interviewer, and advertising spots. The first assignment is the preparation of the scripts. These are corrected and returned, and students are encouraged to rehearse by recording their texts in the laboratory. One class day is then devoted to a "dry run" of the program, and a subsequent day is devoted to the filming. Students are evaluated on their first assignment, their rewrite of the errors noted, their production of French in the assigned role, and the group's final product, their video. If several sections of intermediate French each prepare their own programs, these can be performed for an evening of entertainment with the French Club.

The language of inclusion is a hallmark of the Standards. Indeed, the *Standards'* statement of philosophy—the guiding principles adopted by the steering committee—begins with inclusion: "The United States must educate students who are equipped linguistically and culturally to communicate successfully in a pluralistic American society and abroad. This imperative envisions a future in which ALL students will develop and maintain proficiency in English and at least one other language, modern or classical" (ACTFL, 2014).

While diversity is a prominent characteristic of the *Standards*, and while the authors of the *Standards* maintain that world language educators are typically well prepared to undertake standards development for all students, the learning needs of students with disabilities are not expressly addressed. Yet, as we know, 11% of college students nationwide are students with disabilities.

This oversight begs an important question: Are there elements of world language instructional design that need to be intentionally considered in order to teach *all* students, including students with disabilities?

The French newscast learning scenario, for instance, may take certain nonessential student abilities for granted. For example, is there an assumption that all students will be able to hear and see the newscasts, write or type a script, and interact effectively with others to complete a group project? For a deaf student, a student with a visual impairment, a student on the autism spectrum, or a student with a learning disability, there may be some inherent barriers in the way an instructional task has been designed. To provide a more completely inclusive instruction, to provide opportunities for all students to learn a foreign language, practitioners will need to take a broad range of learners into account.

UNIVERSAL DESIGN FOR INSTRUCTION

With a heightened awareness of the diversity in your classroom and perhaps a new frame for thinking about disability as part of student variation, what does this mean for your instruction? Many language faculty members learning about these concepts for the first time may find themselves thinking, *I've always considered myself a student-centered teacher*, or *my classroom is focused on diverse learners. Have I been excluding students with disabilities?*

Others may wonder, *I provide the disability accommodations the students request. Isn't that enough, or are there strategies I should be using to broaden my teaching?* This is an area where thinking about the learning and cognition of some of our most diverse learners helps educators design instruction that is more inclusive of a broader range of people.

Universal design (UD) is a concept that prompts us to think about diversity and inclusive environments. The idea comes from architecture and the design of physical products. There are examples of UD in the environment all around us. Consider curb cuts; they were designed to make sidewalks more usable by people in wheelchairs, but they also benefit a parent pushing a baby stroller, a teenager on a skateboard, or a business traveler rolling a suitcase. Automatic door openers, captioning on TV screens, and levered door handles are all examples of inclusive design that have become commonplace.

These everyday features in our environment were developed to improve access for people with disabilities and resulted in design that is more usable by many other people as well. This is the core concept of UD.

Using design principles that benefit a broad range of people has obvious appeal for language learning classrooms—not just in the physical environment but extended to classroom instruction as well. The framework of UDI applies these same concepts to college teaching but has been adapted to incorporate concepts from research on college teaching and learning.

Consider this example. When an instructor selects a course textbook that is available in multiple formats such as e-book as well as hard copy, a student who is blind can use a screen reader to read the text without needing to make any additional requests for an accommodation or modified format of the book. Other students may choose to use the electronic format because it is less expensive or less burdensome to carry or because it works best for their personal organization and study strategies.

This instructional element of the language learning classroom is now more usable to a variety of students—providing the equivalent of an instructional curb cut. By providing easy access to this essential learning material, the instructor has already taken an important first step in establishing an inclusive classroom climate even before the first day of classes.

> **STUDENTS SAY**
>
> *Aiden, learning that the instructor uses an online learning management system*: "He posts all documents and allows students to use a laptop computer to take notes in class. I kinda just blend in in that situation."

Source: Scott, Hildebrandt, & Edwards, 2013

Grounded in a social model of disability, UDI begins with awareness of the diversity of students in the classroom. It encourages world language instructors to use this awareness to select approaches to learning and assessment that fit a broad range of learners. Since it is common practice to use multisensory instructional strategies that involve seeing, speaking, listening, and movement, student interaction and small group work are regular features of instruction and assessment of learning. You may, therefore, be asking yourself, *Doesn't this address diverse learning styles? Isn't being attuned to diverse learners just a natural part of good language instruction?*

Good teaching is a subjective experience. Research in the area of college instruction has found that faculty often teach in the way they learned best or in the way their favorite teachers taught. If you experienced lectures as an effective way to learn when you were in graduate school, you are likely to use lectures in your own teaching. If you found fast-paced activities and movement around the classroom to be engaging when you were a student, you will likely draw on these strategies as a teacher in your own classroom. But what worked for you as a successful language learner may be very different from the learning needs of the diverse students in your classroom.

The UDI framework will challenge you to think about a range of student diversity across aspects of the educational environment that you may not have consciously considered in your own learning experience. It will help you increase awareness of possible barriers to learning in the classroom that you perhaps didn't realize existed.

The Nine Principles of UDI

There are nine principles of UDI that provide a framework for designing or revising instruction. (See table 1.2 for a list of the principles.) The principles are general in nature and prompt instructors to think about teaching and possible barriers to learning in the classroom. Since the UDI principles were designed for use across postsecondary disciplines, the authors were curious about their specific application to language learning classrooms.

Table 1.2. The Principles of Universal Design for Instruction Applied to World Language Learning

Principle	Definition
***Principle 1*: Equitable use**	Instruction is designed to be useful to and accessible by people with diverse abilities. Provide the same means of use for all students: identical whenever possible, equivalent when not.
Example: Provide the class syllabus, materials, and links to other resources online. Post the class syllabus online several weeks before classes begin.	
***Principle 2*: Flexibility in use**	Instruction is designed to accommodate a wide range of individual abilities. Provide choice in methods of use.
Example: Use varied instructional methods (verbal information with visual prompts, group activities, use of stories, or web board based discussions) to provide different ways of learning and experiencing knowledge. Switch to a new activity/method every 10 minutes to support attention.	
***Principle 3*: Simple and intuitive**	Instruction is designed in a straightforward and predictable manner, regardless of the student's experience, knowledge, language skills, or current concentration level. Eliminate unnecessary complexity.
Example: Provide a grading rubric that clearly lays out expectations for speaking activities; include information on how expectations for verbal performance will increase over time.	
***Principle 4*: Perceptible information**	Instruction is designed so that necessary information is communicated effectively to the student, regardless of ambient conditions or the student's sensory abilities.
Example: Consider the "readability" of all written documents provided to students. Review instructor-made tests, quizzes, and activities for adequate spacing between items, clear labeling, and easily readable font.	
***Principle 5*: Tolerance for error**	Instruction anticipates variation in individual student learning pace and prerequisite skills.
Example: Anticipate different entry-level skills of students in using the target language. Provide a list of frequently used phrases to support target language use from the first day of class. Clarify that in language acquisition, mistakes are expected as part of the learning process.	
***Principle 6*: Low physical effort**	Instruction is designed to minimize nonessential physical effort in order to allow maximum attention to learning. Note: This principle does not apply when physical effort is integral to essential requirements of a course.

(Continued)

Table 1.2. (Continued)

Principle	Definition
Example: Allow students to use a word processor, tablet, or laptop for writing and editing papers or essay exams. Arrange classroom desks in a semicircle to allow students to see other students speaking during class.	
***Principle 7*: Size and space for approach and use**	Instruction is designed with consideration for appropriate size and space for approach, reach, manipulations, and use regardless of a student's body size, posture, mobility, and communication needs.
Example: Set up group activities that consider the mobility needs of all students. Structure class space (e.g., desk arrangement) or student movement (e.g., rotating group membership) to allow for all students to participate.	
***Principle 8*: A community of learners**	The instructional environment promotes interaction and communication among students and between students and faculty.
Example: Foster communication among students in and out of class by structuring outside cultural activities, language club, or a language table in the dining hall. Use frequent group activities that involve different size and group membership.	
***Principle 9*: Instructional climate**	Instruction is designed to be welcoming and inclusive. High expectations are espoused for all students.
Example: Discuss with students beginning on the first day of class expectations for target language use. Clarify reasonable goals for growth and improvement in target language fluency during the semester.	

Source: Adapted from *Principles of Universal Design for Instruction* by Sally S. Scott, Joan M. McGuire, and Stan F. Shaw (2001). Center on Postsecondary Education and Disability, University of Connecticut.

As part of a larger curriculum development project, the authors worked with a team of very experienced language faculty over a period of one year to examine the UDI principles closely and explore their application to language learning classrooms. We found that some of the principles resonated closely with teaching strategies that are commonly found in language learning classrooms. For example, Principle 2, *flexibility in use*, highlights the importance of using varied instructional methods. This is a hallmark of language learning pedagogy.

Another UDI principle the team of experts identified as frequently present in language learning classrooms is Principle 5, *tolerance for error*. This element speaks to the instructor practice of anticipating the learning tasks that students may find difficult and building in extra supports for those who need additional practice or strategies. A final area where language instructors often excel is Principle 8, *a community of learners*. This principle highlights opportunities for interaction among students and between students and faculty.

While these principles were compatible with frequent instructional practices in language learning classrooms, the team of expert instructors also started to identify some possible barriers to student learning within these typical language learning approaches. For example, can multisensory instruction using a variety of sources of information and experiences become multisensory overload for some students?

Consider, for example, that some students with learning disabilities process information at slower speeds than other students. The student may be very intelligent but may need more time to process spoken information or understand information that is written. This type of uneven learning profile with pockets of weaknesses is characteristic of students with learning disabilities.

Another example of a barrier that came to light when discussing and applying the UDI principles involved activities that are frequently used to promote student community and authentic expression. Does work in small groups or team projects, for example, promote engagement for all students?

Consider students in your classroom who are on the autism spectrum. A primary characteristic of students with this disability diagnosis is difficulty engaging in social interaction. This may create challenges with reading facial expressions, tone of voice, or body language of team members even in the native language. While they are bright and capable of college achievement, their successful participation as a team member on a class assignment will require some new thinking and intentional design on the part of the instructor.

The UDI principles offer a structure for considering these and other barriers to students that can augment more commonly used language learning pedagogy. As you read about the principles, start to think about how these concepts can apply in a variety of ways in your own classroom.

Principle 1, *equitable use*, states the overarching importance of designing your instruction to be accessible to diverse students through identical means whenever possible. For example, when you post the class syllabus and reading materials online, all students in your class have access to that information at the same time. Students can use their own devices, or assistive technology of choice, but the information has been provided for all from the outset.

When you post the class syllabus several weeks before class begins, you increase access even further, allowing the student with a learning disability time to assess whether reading materials are accessible, the student with a chronic health impairment to plan his or her schedule, or the student who is still choosing courses for the term to consider whether an instructor and the class requirements are a good match for his or her learning style.

Principle 2, *flexibility in use*, reminds the language instructor of the importance of presenting material and structuring learning opportunities that allow for student choice. Commonly used textbooks and curricular resources support instructors in providing engaging visual materials such as pictures, videos, and interactive online modules. Activities in class frequently include listening, verbal response, repetition, and movement, offering students a variety of ways to engage and interact with the material they are learning. This is a strength of many language learning classrooms.

Principle 3, *simple and intuitive*, clarifies the importance of removing unnecessary complexity or ambiguity from a learning experience. A good example of this principle is the use of a grading rubric. When students prepare a dialogue for a presentation, or when an exam includes listening and response sections, do students know what is considered exemplary or an "A" level of performance? Grading rubrics help make that expectation more explicit. Note that the focus of this principle is on being straightforward but not changing or lowering standards or expectations.

Principle 4, *perceptible information*, reminds us of the basic concept that information needs to be communicated in a way that is effective and perceptible by students. An obvious example of this principle would be providing reading materials for a student who has a vision impairment. With advances in technology, the simple process of providing materials in electronic format in advance allows students to use their own assistive technology to "read" or "view" the materials.

Beyond this basic sensory perception, the principle prompts us to think about other types of perception as well. As you juggle the many responsibilities of teaching and being a faculty member, do you ever find yourself quickly formulating a quiz for tomorrow's class? It may be tempting to quickly write out or make edits to the quiz in your own handwriting. But consider that you likely have students in your class with ADHD or LD that affect reading. The principle of perceptible information encourages us to be aware that irregular text and uneven spacing can cause barriers for some students.

Principle 5, *tolerance for error*, reminds the language instructor to be attuned to the different background experiences and learning pace of the diverse students in the classroom. It also prompts instructors to learn from their own teaching experience, observing where students have difficulty in the curriculum and building in additional resources and opportunities to practice and master difficult concepts.

In the language classroom, as students continue to build vocabulary and simultaneously practice verbal communication, it is not uncommon for students to experience times when they don't know or have forgotten a specific word they are seeking. Encouraging students to use circumlocution to express the concept in the absence of the specific vocabulary word is a good example of a frequently used strategy in language classrooms to help students with a common learning challenge. This is the concept of tolerance for error.

Principle 6, *low physical effort*, focuses the instructor's attention on the physical elements of the classroom. Are there distractions or barriers that, if removed, would promote student focus and attention to learning? For example, students who are hard of hearing often rely on lip reading and facial expressions in spoken conversations. Is it possible to arrange the seating in the classroom in a semicircle so all students can see the faces of all speakers? If your classroom has fluorescent lights, do they have a humming sound or do they flicker? Some students with ADHD find this incredibly distracting; students on the autism spectrum may have sound or light sensitivity that make this very challenging to tune out and focus on learning.

Principle 7, *size and space for approach and use*, is another principle that prompts the instructor to think about the classroom environment. As you design different activities for learning, will all students be able to move and participate in all projects and tasks? Be attuned to the demands on student mobility. Is there adequate space for a student in a wheelchair to navigate the aisles? Do small group activities allow sufficient time for all students to shift locations or seating?

Principle 8, *community of learners*, prompts language instructors to build on this strong element of language learning pedagogy. Small group breakout activities, games, skits, and dialogues all provide opportunities for student connection. Frequent verbal exchange and feedback between a student and faculty member also contribute to a sense of classroom community. This principle prompts the instructor to assure that these interactions are inclusive of all students in the class.

Principle 9, *instructional climate*, serves as a reminder that the language learning classroom should be welcoming and inclusive. High expectations for learning are clearly communicated to all students. This principle warrants particular examination related to students with disabilities who for a variety of reasons may have experienced barriers to language learning in the past. As part of a larger research project, the authors conducted focus groups with students with disabilities. One of the factors students mentioned as helpful in making the instructor more approachable and welcoming was a simple statement in the class syllabus inviting students to come see the instructor during office hours to discuss learning needs.

The nine principles of UDI are provided here for your reference along with some illustrative examples that relate to language learning. These principles and their applications are the foundation for the strategies we share with you in this book. You can return to the UDI principles over time as you continue to explore inclusive strategies in your classroom. Throughout the remainder of this book, we will focus on specific tips and strategies that will guide you through essential aspects of your language learning classroom. But this is the framework you can return to over time as you expand your approaches to inclusive teaching.

Reflection

- In which ways do the principles of UDI speak to the values of world language instructors?
- In which ways do the UDI principles suggest solutions to specific, chronic teaching dilemmas?

SUMMARY

This chapter lays the foundation for designing an inclusive language learning classroom. With heightened awareness about many forms of student diversity, including students with a variety of disabilities, you can begin to examine *student-centered* teaching in a new light. We hope you have gained a new appreciation for how a social model of disability shifts the focus of teaching from making exceptions for students with disabilities to identifying barriers in the instructional environment. The chapter concludes with an overview of the principles of UDI, the framework that helps instructors tap into the power of designing inclusive language learning classrooms.

Chapter 2 examines the fundamental elements of course development and planning in the world language classroom. Following strategies for proactive planning, you will be guided through brief case studies that encourage your own critical thinking about application of the strategies in your classroom.

Chapter 2

Setting the Stage for an Inclusive Language Learning Classroom

One of the hallmarks of becoming a more inclusive teacher is to embrace the role of instructor as a *designer* of the class. In addition to traditional conceptions of teacher as educator, scholar, trainer, or mentor, being a designer highlights the importance of proactive and intentional planning.

This chapter begins the work of designing by examining the basic infrastructure of the class well before students arrive. After exploring the familiar elements of the physical layout of the classroom, selection and development of instructional materials, and components of the class syllabus, the chapter concludes with a look at instructor disposition and the important role it plays for diverse learners. Infusing inclusive strategies in these foundational elements of the class helps "set the stage," both literally and figuratively for a welcoming and inclusive classroom environment.

CLASSROOM SETUP

Because universal design originated in assessments of the built environment, the physical setup of the classroom is a good place to begin any evaluation of inclusive world language instruction. Anticipating student diversity naturally leads instructors to gauge the very makeup of the room itself—not the strengths, weaknesses, and personalities of the individual students but the strengths, weakness, and personality of the space where instruction happens.

From a physical perspective you may be asking yourself, *Why does the classroom set-up matter? This isn't middle school. These are adult students.* Or you may be wondering, *I am assigned a room in which to teach. How much control do I have about the environment?*

To address these questions and to learn more about environmental and other barriers to learning, the authors interviewed students with disabilities as part of a large research project. The students had different types of cognitive and physical disabilities. They had completed high school language requirements and experienced between one and six semesters of language coursework at the college level. One of the barriers to learning that these students addressed was the set-up of the classroom and how it affected their communication with the instructor and with classmates.

STUDENTS SAY

Ahmed on the arrangement of desks: "The actual layout of the class was more of a round circle. . . . It felt comfortable to be able to just see everyone's reaction to something or have the professor there but not standing in front of you overlooking you."

Source: Scott, Hildebrandt, & Edwards, 2013

While classrooms come in all shapes and sizes, instructors do have some control over particular elements of the physical environment. Taking maximum advantage of the relatively small size of most world language classes can go a long way toward creating an atmosphere of community, communication, interaction, and inclusion.

Even something as simple as the arrangement of the students' desks can play a role in students' perception of the class. Desks arranged in traditional rows, for instance, direct everyone's attention to the front of the room, creating a focused environment for imparting and receiving information but making conversation more difficult. Desks arranged in pods or semicircles, by contrast, facilitate interaction and natural conversation but can also lead to unfocused clutter and noise.

Designing an inclusive classroom requires instructors to pay attention not only to the requirements of a particular lesson but also to the needs of individual students within the context of the instructional setting. World language classes are classes in interactive communication, where speaking, listening, reading, and writing all play a vital part in learning. It is important that students be able to hear one other, to see one another, and to network with one another. How can the instructor manipulate the physical environment to maximize learning in these three areas? Let's look at them individually.

An inclusive classroom is one in which all students can hear well. Since most communication happens in the target language, it always takes extra effort for students to comprehend the spoken word. Instructors must speak deliberately and loudly. Even in the best circumstances, video segments or lab exercises must be repeated several times to assure students grasp meaning. Inferences, cues, shortcuts, and supports that all students use in their first language to make sense of spoken communication are rarely available in the second language.

The physical environment can enhance or hinder a student's ability to hear the target language well. A classroom with high ceilings and heavy reverberation, for instance, impedes the clear distinction of sounds and may provide barriers to learning. A classroom of 20 students, but with seats for 50, might also complicate a student's ability to hear well if the class is spread throughout the room. Fixed desks or theater-style chairs can make it difficult for students to face their partner during conversation exercises.

These architectural limitations can, nonetheless, be overcome if the instructor is attuned to them. For example, students in a large classroom can be asked to sit close together. Student responses can be repeated succinctly by the instructor for all to hear. Students can be instructed to turn to the group when they speak rather than to the instructor. In short, anticipating student diversity and including students who are hard of hearing require the instructor to take stock of the educational setting and adapt it where possible to facilitate learning.

STUDENTS SAY

Joel on classroom chemistry: "You need to feel like there's some sort of membership there and break down that barrier . . . between students and between students and teachers."

Source: Scott, Hildebrandt, & Edwards, 2010

Lighting is another element of the physical space that instructors are able to manipulate in the interests of inclusive teaching. It may be obvious that bright lighting is necessary during most interactive, reading, or writing exercises and that low lighting is beneficial when slides or videos are projected on a screen. However, in a dynamic world language classroom that regularly moves from one activity to another, the lighting should rarely stay static.

Low lighting can make it difficult to read writing on a white board, as can a marker that is running out of ink. For a student with visual impairments, incorrect lighting can thwart standard compensating skills, compound a disability, and hinder learning.

Imagine, for example, that morning sunlight streaming in a window washes out the slide projected on a screen. Students without visual impairments may, nevertheless, be able to distinguish some information and ascertain meaning. Students with vision disabilities, on the other hand, might struggle to see any image at all. An inclusive instructor will not only lower the lights to aid projection but will also lower the shades and create high-contrast slides.

A classroom space that facilitates adequate hearing and seeing is critical regardless of the discipline. Unlike other college disciplines, though, world language classrooms also require constant physical movement. On a daily basis, students will turn to their partners to work on an activity that requires them to gather information from a partner or mingle with the whole class to conduct a poll or participate in a networking exercise to practice asking questions.

In the course of facilitating these typical activities, inclusive instructors will reflect on the potential barriers caused by the learning space. Is it possible for all students to navigate throughout the room? A wheelchair user or a student with crutches may provoke obvious accommodations, but students with less visible disabilities may also benefit from proactive manipulation of the built environment. For instance, haphazard furniture can impede even fully mobile students from circulating freely, while a student with a cast may find it impossible to poll classmates while also writing down responses.

A student with a psychological disability or social anxiety who finds forced interaction debilitating in any language may struggle even further in a cramped space ill-suited to the task at hand. Creating useful space by moving desks to the walls of the room or moving students to the front of the room or moving the entire class into the hallway is a possible strategy to adapting a learning space that does not quite match the needs of the lesson.

Reflection

Pause for a minute and think about the classroom(s) you will be teaching in this term.

- What elements of the classroom environment can you control?
- What do you need to consider to make sure that all students can hear one another, see one another, and network with one another?

With these physical elements of the classroom environment in mind, it's time to start applying the principles of UDI. The case study that follows describes a typical classroom interaction. What barriers do you see and how could the instructor modify his classroom practices to be more inclusive?

CASE STUDY 2.1: A CHILLING ICEBREAKER

It is the first day of classes, and Professor Salinas is feeling confident about starting his second year as a tenure-track faculty member at Johnson State University. He enjoys teaching the introductory language courses, and his Spanish 102 section has full student enrollment this semester. As he walks down the hall to the classroom, he thinks about the energy of the students on the first day of class. His main goal today is to start to connect with his students and build their sense of community in the course. It will be important to get them talking and sharing right off the bat.

Professor Salinas welcomes the class with some introductory comments. Just as he finishes going over the syllabus, a student in a wheelchair comes blustering in. "Sorry! The elevator was tied up and I had to wait for it." Professor Salinas pulls a chair away from the only unoccupied desk in the room and invites the student, Angie, to join them. He thinks to himself, "Whew. Glad the chairs are movable—that was an easy fix for rolling up her wheelchair."

As Angie gets settled, Professor Salinas introduces the first activity, an ice breaker that he uses to get students up and moving. "*Bueno*, let's get to know one another and review how to introduce ourselves. Take a look at the list of categories on the white board. Get up, circulate around the room and talk with one another. Find someone who meets each of the descriptors listed up here: someone from out of state, someone who traveled abroad this summer, and on down the list." Students slowly start interacting, and Professor Salinas notices that the buzz of conversation in the room is increasing.

At first Angie talks with the students on either side of her, but as they shift and start to circulate to others in the room, she finds herself stranded. She is boxed in by chairs that have been pulled away from the desks and are now scattered haphazardly. As Professor Salinas moves around the room and talks with students, he notices Angie and goes over and sits down beside her. "Tell me about yourself . . ." and they have a nice conversation.

When time is up, Professor Salinas returns to the front of the class and announces, "Time to wrap up your conversations and return to your seats."

Reflection Questions

1. Was this icebreaker activity an equitable learning opportunity for Angie?
2. What were the barriers Angie encountered in the physical space? (Hint: the barrier is *not* the wheelchair!)
3. What were the barriers Angie experienced in the design of the activity? (Hint: the barrier is *still* not the wheelchair!)
4. What did you think of Professor Salinas's response to support Angie by sitting down and talking with her? Was his approach helpful in making a connection with Angie? Was it helpful in connecting her with other students?

UDI Resolution

It may be easy to overlook the importance of physical space when preparing for student learning. In Angie's case, however, the environment clearly plays a significant role in how she is able to participate in class and connect with her classmates. Being delayed in getting to class, missing the instructor's opening comments and syllabus overview, and being physically sidelined from a class activity are not an equitable first day of class!

What are the barriers in this scenario? In the past, a traditional approach to planning for disability access would suggest the barrier is the student's inability to walk. Under the old model or the medical model described in chapter 1, you might assume that the stairs in the building provide access to the second-floor classroom for most students; similarly, asking students to circulate in the room for the icebreaker activity works for most students. But in an inclusive classroom, the goal is to design instruction for broad student diversity. Is it equitable for the ability to walk and climb stairs to play a role in Angie's participation in Spanish 102?

As absurd as this question may sound, these barriers still exist on college campuses, often because we overlook the impact of the physical space on students in our classrooms. The universal design framework prompts the instructor to shift the focus from identifying the student's disability as the problem to intentionally thinking about the design of the environment and the potential barriers to student learning. Three UDI principles give us direction in this case.

The UDI principle addressing *size and space for approach and use* (see Principle 7 in table 1.2) calls for the instructor to consider how students engage in the class regardless of factors such as student mobility, body size, posture, or communication needs. As you design your class, ask yourself:

- Can all students physically enter and function in the classroom?
- Can all students participate in the learning opportunities and instructional activities as they have been designed?

In Angie's case, applying this principle reveals several possible environmental barriers, including the following:

- Reliable access to upper floors of the building
- Seating in the classroom that is usable
- Participation in class activities that involve student movement

Some of the barriers can be addressed directly by the instructor. Consider the icebreaker activity. Are there ways the students can mingle with one another while providing open areas for movement? Solutions might be as simple as adding one more step of instruction, directing all students to push in their chairs or move all chairs to the edges of the room before the activity begins. This will allow Angie to circulate among other students. It may also benefit other students in the class who are large in stature or perhaps older than traditional-age students and experience difficulty with mobility.

Other barriers in the environment may be beyond your direct control. Consider the delay Angie experienced with the elevator. This may be a one-time inconvenience. But what if the elevator is "out of service" on a frequent basis? While building access is not an instructor's responsibility, consider contacting the staff at the campus disability resource office and letting them know the barrier exists. (See chapter 5 for more information about work and collaboration with your campus disability resource office.)

Another UDI principle relates to building *a community of learners* (see Principle 8 in table 1.2). In the scenario, Professor Salinas clearly has this idea in mind when he includes an icebreaker activity on the first day of classes. Addressing the physical layout of the room, however, will assure the icebreaker is structured to include more diverse students in community building. Chapter 3 explores other types of barriers and design solutions to building a community of learners in group activities.

When Professor Salinas notices that Angie is isolated in the class activity, he responds by sitting down and having a more lengthy conversation with her while the other students complete the activity. On the one hand, Professor Salinas is recognizing Angie is excluded from the mingling activity and uses the moment to build a connection with her. On the other hand, Angie is well aware that she is an outlier in the class.

A UDI principle that Professor Salinas will need to address going forward in the class is related to *instructional climate* (see Principle 9 in table 1.2). Now that he is aware of some of the barriers that inadvertently occurred on the first day of class, he can review and tweak his lesson plans to anticipate future physical demands of the classroom setup and create a more welcoming environment.

INSTRUCTIONAL MATERIALS: ARE THEY ACCESSIBLE?

A second foundational aspect of planning a course is to consider and select instructional materials. Given the course objectives and desired outcomes, what textbook is best suited to provide the core of the curriculum content? What supporting materials are available to give students additional exposure and opportunities to practice or expand what they are learning? What other kinds of engaging activities, visuals, and experiences will you incorporate into the course? Will you choose videos and films? Short stories or poems? Authentic artifacts or realia such as train schedules or maps? These important materials enliven instruction and student engagement in a variety of ways.

In addition, technology has revolutionized how we think about and provide instructional materials. The lines between face-to-face classroom learning and online learning have blurred.

Institutional learning management systems (LMSs), such as Moodle, Canvas, or Desire2Learn, are common platforms for class websites. Online workbooks are the norm. Homework and practice programs, such as Kahoot and Gimkit, expand opportunities for students to engage in learning on their phones outside class. The Internet itself offers limitless ways to introduce and experience culture, so, for example, the French website for the Eiffel Tower or the Louvre could be used with instructor-created materials to provide authentic and engaging materials.

The variety of media and opportunities to share this learning with students is exciting and a hallmark of the multisensory instruction often found in language learning classes. But, as we think about providing access for more diverse learners, consider also the possible challenges. Sometimes the format of instructional materials presents a barrier. Do the materials you've chosen or developed assume all students can see a computer screen, hear the narrative in a video, type responses on the keyboard, or decode printed text? These assumptions may be true for many students but not all.

So what can you do? It can be overwhelming as you start to think about the range of materials and formats. Two of the UDI principles provide guidance for making materials more accessible. First, consider whether your materials are *perceptible by students with different sensory abilities* (see Principle 4 in table 1.2). For example, how would a student who is blind use the textbook? How would a student who has hearing loss experience a film? And since students vary so widely, even among students who have the same disability label, the principles prompt us to build in *flexibility and choice* (UDI Principle 2) in how to access instructional materials.

Quick Starting Points

Applying these two UDI principles, here are some quick starting points as you plan your course. There are some things you can do immediately that will help.

- Make textbook and supplemental resource decisions early in the course registration period and post this on the website. Include the ISBN number.
- If you are teaching an upper-level language course that requires other reading materials, provide a complete list of assigned reading, including due dates and specific pages numbers, as early as possible.
- Request that the bookstore include e-book formats of your text and supplemental resources as an option if available.
- Plan to use the institution's LMS rather than a personal website to host your class webpage so you can benefit from the accessible online features that are available.
- Upload your syllabus to the course website. Create the syllabus as an HTML page in the LMS for greater accessibility.
- Post instructional materials and lecture materials such as PowerPoint slides on the class website in advance of class and as early as possible. Whenever possible, post these materials in multiple electronic formats such as Word, PDF, and RTF. This will allow students to choose the format that works best for them.
- Select videos or films that have closed captioning. If not captioned, is a transcript available? If not, contact the disability services office as early as possible to discuss alternatives.

The focus of most of these quick starting points is on making materials available in electronic format. This is typically the easiest and most flexible format for students to access with their assistive technology, including supports such as text enlargement, screen readers, or notetaking. By providing materials well in advance, you are building in time for students to arrange for document conversion to other formats if needed.

These quick tips help students in getting timely accommodations. To build on this foundation, consider the other materials you use throughout the course, including quizzes, tests, activities, and handouts. Did you know that documents in Microsoft Word or PDF format are sometimes difficult or impossible for assistive technology to "read"? Were you aware that the images in PowerPoint slides are not detected by screen readers?

As more students access instructional materials using different technology and media for a variety of reasons including disability access, it is important to increase your awareness of some simple ways to make your materials more usable and accessible for students. In chapter 5, we will talk about building your skills to design documents in more accessible formats.

Reflection

Do a quick mental scan of the instructional materials you typically use in class.

- How accessible are your instructional materials?
- What is the best starting point for you in reviewing your materials and assuring you are providing them in accessible ways?

AN INCLUSIVE SYLLABUS

The course syllabus remains the key document for communicating an instructor's expectations, disposition, and values. No matter how much forethought you devote to the design of the course content, the accessibility of key materials, or the physical environment of the classroom, the syllabus—as an extension of the instructor's personality and principles—can be an important early signal to students about the inclusive nature of your pedagogy.

There is often great variation in how faculty members design their syllabi. Whether it's a 1-page flyer that announces due dates and a list of required materials or a 15-page catalog of prompts, rubrics, links to campus resources, and a day-by-day schedule, the course syllabus is always a complicated document. Both ends of the spectrum—both the minimal document and the exhaustive tome—present potential barriers for students.

For example, did you know that students with ADHD often need to work closely with a personal calendar to schedule time for assignments and begin longer-term projects well in advance? Did you realize that some students have disabilities that require readings in alternative formats such as Braille, enlarged print, or e-text?

Converting reading materials may require advanced preparation to assure reading is available to students with disabilities in a timely way. For these students, a more "emergent" approach to class, such as the one-page syllabus, can present barriers that prevent access to essential learning and organizational strategies. Students with reading difficulties, on the other hand, may experience the 15-page syllabus as information overload. Therefore, how does an instructor strike a balance in creating an inclusive syllabus?

The syllabus is a contract between the student and the university. It must include ordinary, foundational information, such as the instructor's name and contact information. It may include grading guidelines and an attendance policy. It should spell out meeting times and assignments. Much of this foundational information—and even the way that information appears on the page or screen—may be uniform throughout a department, particularly if a course includes several different sections taught by several different instructors.

This is particularly true of world language courses. Since students move from one course to another within a scaffolded sequence, there will often be a high degree of cohesion in the way classroom requirements are determined and presented to students at the beginning of the semester.

Moreover, because beginning- and intermediate-level language courses are increasingly staffed by graduate teaching assistants, part-time adjunct instructors, or full-time, non-tenure-track lecturers, the syllabus may actually be more of a template created by a supervisor, increasing overall uniformity but reducing instructor choice. Nonetheless, even with considerable uniformity, it is still possible to infuse a course syllabus with inclusive principles.

To be truly inclusive, consider three areas when drafting a syllabus before the semester begins:

1. Does the syllabus specifically anticipate students with disabilities?
2. Does the syllabus foster a professional, welcoming environment by balancing details of essential information with a concern for overkill?
3. Is the document designed to be easy to read and visually appealing?

To address the first question, two simple tasks can help students with disabilities understand that their presence in the classroom is not a surprise or afterthought but is, indeed, expected and welcome. The first task is to include a disability statement in the syllabus that makes students aware of campus resources and invites them to discuss their learning directly with the instructor.

This is the statement used at Longwood University: "If you have a disability and require accommodations, please meet with me early in the semester to discuss your learning needs. If you wish to request reasonable accommodations (notetaking support, extended time for tests, etc.), you will need to register with the Office of Disability Resources. The office will require appropriate documentation of disability. All information is kept confidential."

Including a simple statement that acknowledges disability at such an important time in the semester will not only help alleviate potential anxiety on the part of the student but also help the student practice the skills of self-advocacy needed to make a smooth transition from the high school classroom to the postsecondary environment.

A second quick task to consider is the way the syllabus will be delivered to students. The traditional method is to distribute paper copies while discussing policies and due dates on the first day of the class. Online classroom management systems have fortunately made it easy to deliver the syllabus in multiple formats, allowing students to choose the one that best suits their needs. Many will access the syllabus from a screen, whether on a computer or smartphone, which provides easy convenience. The ability to read a syllabus on a screen, however, also accommodates a student with a visual impairment, who would otherwise need the paper document resized or read aloud.

Adding a disability statement to a syllabus that is available in several formats already sends a signal to students that the instructor is aware that the class roll is comprised of a variety of diverse learners. An instructor can further demonstrate this awareness by drafting a syllabus that provides a substantial outline of the course without overwhelming the reader with details. Electronic formats can again be useful in this regard.

Imagine a course in intermediate German that will require the student to write a series of short compositions throughout the semester. Some students may be interested to know the subject of those compositions very early in the semester, even if the due date is weeks away. Others may not need that information until they begin to write the assignment. Still other students may want to know how the compositions will be graded. A final group may want to be sure they understand how the writing portion of the class compares to the spoken portion in the overall final grade.

While it would be possible to include all this information in the syllabus, the risk of drowning learners in details or unintentionally burying more immediately important information is high. An online syllabus would allow the instructor to meet the divergent needs of all these students simultaneously.

Perhaps the main document would sketch the basic components and weights of the composition category, while links to other documents would make additional information available when the students wish to access it. Self-advocacy skills would again come into play; students would be responsible for gathering information when it is most timely for them. In addition, because the syllabus can be used in multiple ways and is thus useful to a variety of learners, the instructor reinforces a welcoming and flexible pedagogy while maintaining a balance in the presentation of vital information.

A third area to consider in the creation of a course syllabus is the visual design and tone of the document itself. Keeping in mind that the syllabus must establish basic contractual expectations, it is also an extension of the demeanor and values of the instructor. A syllabus with tables and graphs that are easy to scan helps students find and digest information quickly (see, e.g., textbox 2.1). One that highlights major elements with a bold font or distinct headings easily distinguishes elements that could otherwise run together.

In contrast, a syllabus that includes flashing icons or random font changes or garish colors may end up concealing information with clutter. A syllabus that admonishes students in capital letters with threats of failure for missed classes or honor code violations may negate any goodwill accrued by careful planning.

TEXTBOX 2.1   SYLLABUS EXAMPLES

These two examples of syllabus content contain the same information. The second example reflects a visual layout that is more straightforward for students.

Example 1:

Evaluación: Your grade will be based on many factors. Participación (*class participation and online participation*) 10%, Ensayos (*essays and written assignments*) 5%, Pruebitas (*quizzes*), Tarea: iLrn (*homework, book, online lab and workbook, individual page*) 15%, Exámenes parciales (*partial exams*) 30%, Producción oral (*oral exam + other oral exercises, including individual page*) 10%, Examen final (*final exam*) 20%.

Example 2:

Evaluación—SPAN 102

Participación (*class participation and online participation*)	10%
Ensayos (*essays and written assignments*)	5%
Pruebitas (*quizzes*)	10%
Tarea: iLrn (*homework, book, online lab and workbook, individual page*)	15%
Exámenes parciales (*partial exams*)	30%
Producción oral (*oral exam + other oral exercises, including individual page*)	10%
Examen final (*final exam*)	20%
Total	100%

Reflection

Take a minute to review your current syllabus from a perspective of accessibility.

- Have you included a disability access statement?
- What is your overall tone in the syllabus? Are you creating the climate for learning that you hope to achieve?
- Is the layout straightforward and simple to understand?

With these elements of the syllabus in mind, we turn to another case study. What barriers have been created by the syllabus in this scenario? Think about the UDI principles and how they might inform your response.

CASE STUDY 2.2: A WHOLE NEW WORLD

Professor Ballestra hits the save button, closes the document on her computer screen, and leans back in her chair. She has finally had a chance to make the remaining edits to her syllabus for French 101. She has taught the class in previous semesters, but she really wanted to tweak some of her assignments and try out some new ways to give students feedback about their work this term.

But things had been crazy for several weeks before the fall semester this year. Professor Ballestra had a manuscript that had come back from the editor with a "revise and resubmit" request, and those edits had to be made quickly. There was a new professional development requirement for the department and mandatory workshops to attend. And, of course, this was when her son needed his wisdom teeth removed, and that had required a little extra TLC on the home front.

Professor Ballestra was done with the syllabus now, though, and it was the third week of classes. She took a sip of hot tea and made plans to post the syllabus on the course website. Next, she would send an electronic copy over to the department office for their files. "At least it will be submitted before the department deadline," she thinks to herself.

There was a light knock on her door, and she sees a student in the doorway.

"Hi, Professor Ballestra. My name is Janay Klein. I'm in your French 101 class."

"Yes, of course, Janay. Come in. I'm glad you found me during office hours. How are things going?"

"Well, my mom said I should come talk to you about my 504 for your class," explains Janay. "I need to have reduced homework assignments because I have ADHD, and the assignments take me a long time to do. And I'll also need more time for tests and quizzes, so I just wanted to be sure you knew."

After a slight pause, Professor Ballestra says "Hmmmm. . . . Okay. . . . So, let's back up a minute. I'm not quite following you. You mentioned a 504? I'm not sure what that means."

"Oh," Janay says sounding slightly flustered. "You know, um, the document that says what the school is required to do for me so I can learn. It's the law. You have to do those things for my ADHD."

"Okay," Professor Ballestra says slowly as she takes a calming breath and makes a mental note to herself that she needs to connect Janay with the disability resource office on campus. "Tell me more about this homework request. How has the homework gone for you so far in my class? Have you had any trouble completing the online workbook assignments?"

"Well, actually, I was kind of confused about that. I know you wrote some homework on the board, and I did write it down, but when I went to look for it, I wasn't sure where I'd written it. And so, I haven't been able to work on it yet," Janay explains. "But homework usually takes me a lot longer than everybody else."

"I see. Well, I think a good first step for you is to get connected with the disability resource office here on campus. Accommodations and services work a little differently at the college level, and they will be able to tell you what you need to do for that. You should do this right away so we can get things in place for you."

"Okay," Janay says nodding. "I think I've seen that office over in the Student Center. It's beside the tutoring center, right?"

"Yes, that's the one," Professor Ballestra confirms. "And I think this will help you too. I've just finished the syllabus for our class," she explains as she opens the document on her screen and selects the print function. "Here's a hardcopy, and it has all of the homework assignments laid out for the semester. I'm also putting it on our class website, so you can find it there too. Give the assignments a try and let me know if you have any trouble with them."

"Okay, I can do that," Janay responds.

"And Janay, let me know how it goes with the disability resource office, okay?"

"Okay. Thanks, Professor Ballestra. See you in class tomorrow."

Reflection Questions

1. What were the barriers that Janay experienced?
2. What were some of the strengths in the way Janay approached Professor Ballestra?
3. How would access to the syllabus on the first day of class possibly have changed Janay's first encounters with French 101 in college?

UDI Resolution

There are certainly times in faculty work when everything seems to come due at once. Managing the multiple expectations for teaching, research, and service is the challenging nature of the profession. The beginning of a new academic year is particularly prone to long and busy days as students return and the work of the institution gears up again. You may be thinking, *With everything else on my plate, is the timing of the syllabus a big deal?* In the scenario with Janay, we see that the lack of a syllabus may be more than just an inconvenience.

What are the barriers for Janay in this scenario? Your first response may be to think that Janay's lack of awareness about resources and organization is the problem. *Why didn't she know about the disability resource office? Don't the high schools help students get ready for this transition to college?* And when Janay says that she has lost the homework assignments, did you find yourself thinking, *and next it will be the dog ate my homework? Come on. You're in college now!* Looking more closely at the environment gives us a different perspective, however.

Two UDI principles are particularly relevant. The principle that relates to *tolerance for error* (see Principle 5 in table 1.2) prompts the instructor to consider aspects of the course that may be challenging for students and then to build in supports. As you design or modify your class, ask yourself:

- Are there elements of the course where I can predict that some students may have difficulty?
- How can I build in resources, information, or support that will help address this challenge?

In this case study, one of the environmental barriers for Janay was the lack of information about how to receive accommodations for the class. With 11% of college students disclosing a disability, the instructor can predict that this is important information to include on every syllabus.

The resolution is easy; include a disability statement such as the one described earlier in the syllabus and provide this on the first day of class.

Janay is still responsible for following through with the university's procedures for contacting the disability resource office and requesting accommodations, but with earlier notice, she will have the information she needs to self-advocate in a timelier way.

Another relevant UDI principle highlights the importance of making instruction *simple and intuitive* (see Principle 3 in table 1.2). In the case study, Professor Ballestra knows there is a plan for a regular homework schedule that complements the weekly class activities. She has written the assignments on the board at the end of each class meeting. Perhaps she has verbally reminded students about the homework as they are gathering their materials to leave at the end of class. How does writing the daily assignment on the board for the first several class meetings introduce more complexity and possible barriers for Janay?

Consider some typical characteristics of ADHD and their possible impact in this situation:

- Difficulty with attention to detail (Did Janay copy the assignment correctly?)
- Challenges with organization (Did Janay have a planner, app, or notebook for keeping track of the assignment, or did she jot it down on a scrap of paper that she has since misplaced?)
- Weakness in auditory working memory (Did Janay hear the reminder from Professor Ballestra and quickly forget?)
- Difficulty with executive functioning. This term refers to the brain's ability to effectively plan and complete tasks. (Did Janay understand that these homework assignments would be a regular and ongoing part of learning for the class?)

Each of these barriers can be addressed, at least to some extent, by providing the syllabus, including the complete list of homework assignments, on the first day of classes. Giving the students the syllabus in electronic format enhances access even further. Providing this structure early and in multiple formats makes learning and homework completion a more straightforward task for all students.

While recognizing possible barriers for Janay, it's also helpful to notice the strengths she demonstrated in this scenario. She took the initiative to reach out to the instructor and used the appropriate schedule of visiting during Professor Ballestra's office hours. She told the professor she had a disability that affected her learning in the class and would need accommodations. These are all behaviors that are sometimes hard for first-year students with disabilities. Professor Ballestra made the conversation easier by being welcoming, asking questions, and referring the student to institutional channels.

Will Janay receive all of the accommodations she thinks are "required"? Reduced homework assignments are typically not an accommodation provided at the college level. When Janay talks with the staff at the disability resource office, they will likely tell her that accommodations are not always the same in high school and college because the learning contexts are so different. Instead of reducing the homework, the staff will likely suggest strategies to help Janay meet deadlines. They may suggest she start homework early to allow more time, block time nightly if needed on her schedule, and use campus supports such as the tutoring center or language lab.

Some campuses offer one-to-one support for students who need to build their planning skills. Some students with ADHD hire private academic coaches to help them develop this scheduling and prioritizing skill. The inclusive college instructor's role is to make the assignments and requirements simple to understand, but there is no expectation of reducing requirements or expectations for student learning.

INSTRUCTOR DISPOSITION

A final design element, and perhaps the most important feature of an inclusive classroom, is the instructor's own disposition. "Instructor disposition" refers to the many tangible and intangible ways the professor conveys an attitude about teaching and working with students. Creating a welcoming classroom that encourages interaction among students and between students and faculty hinges on this critical element. In research interviewing students with disabilities, the authors discovered that instructor characteristics, in fact, play an outsized role in effectiveness of a world language class.

Perhaps unsurprisingly, students appreciated the learning environment created by instructors who are flexible, focused, and easy to communicate with outside of class. They also valued someone who speaks the target language at a reasonable pace, leaves room for student errors, and provides moments of respite from the target language. (We will talk more about strategies to support target language use in chapter 3.) Likewise, an instructor with clear expectations—a syllabus with explicit assignment pages and due dates, for instance—helped students navigate the semester.

Students with disabilities appreciated instructors who were approachable and made it easy to initiate a conversation about accommodations. They were aware of institutional procedures and responded in an informed way when the student presented the faculty notification letter about accommodation requests for the class. In other words, they made it easy for students to be effective self-advocates.

> **STUDENTS SAY**
>
> *Devon on instructor disposition:* "I had one that I just couldn't talk to. I couldn't talk to the teacher. She was very unwelcoming."

Source: Scott, Hildebrandt, & Edwards, 2013

While interviewees offered many comments about positive and desirable attributes of teachers, there were two areas of professor disposition that students noted as creating barriers. Faculty members who were not approachable were the primary concern. Consider the dilemma this creates for students with disabilities who are charged with disclosing a disability and discussing accommodations that are needed. A student who is new to the self-advocacy required in college may be unsure of how to respond to instructors who are unaware of their responsibilities or who react negatively to the student's disclosure of a disability.

> **STUDENTS SAY**
>
> *Mikayla on instructor reaction to accommodations*: "There were teachers that I didn't have a problem with, but there are a few bad eggs that I still, every time I go [*to request accommodations*] I still go into it kind of fearing that there might be issues."

Source: Scott, Hildebrandt, & Edwards, 2013

A second barrier discussed by students were those faculty members who had perhaps unreasonably high expectations for students. Student anxiety about faculty expectations in language learning is not unique to students with disabilities. There is certainly ample research about the interconnected nature of student anxiety, motivation, and language learning achievement that makes the importance of instructor disposition for all students quite apparent. Knowing that your affect in the language classroom carries special weight, what steps could you consider to help bridge this barrier?

Perhaps the most important step is to learn who your students are. Recognizing that effective pedagogy is determined by the needs of the learner, inclusive teachers always begin by "reading the room." If you are new to the faculty or teaching on campus for the first time, talk with the program chair and other colleagues about the student body. Generally, why do they study a second language and what connections would be helpful to make with other disciplines or interests? What strategies do they use to connect with students and make the classroom a comfortable learning environment?

In addition to learning about students as a demographic, it can be revealing and beneficial to ask your specific students, early in the term, to reflect on their world language learning. An exercise in metacognition, where students think about how they approach a world language class, can provide real insights to both students and instructors. This exercise may then foster a conversation about learning strategies and about the purposes of learning a second language in the first place. Asking students both how they learn and why they learn a second language can help foster a team mind-set and set expectations for the semester.

One such activity is a quick, one-page questionnaire that first asks students to list their strengths and weakness as a general student and then asks them to connect those strengths and weaknesses to the language classroom. You might also ask students to describe their favorite characteristics of a world language instructor and their pet peeves in the classroom.

Asking students to complete the prompt "To me, learning a foreign language is like . . ." often generates engaging discussions with students. Look at the examples of student responses generated by this prompt and provided in textbox 2.2. What do these student metaphors tell you about their perceptions of language learning? What might you glean about student expectations and possible anxiety levels coming into your class? How might you need to modulate your disposition to respond to the student mind-set that is revealed with these responses?

TEXTBOX 2.2   SAMPLE STUDENT RESPONSES TO THE PROMPT: "FOR ME LEARNING A FOREIGN LANGUAGE IS LIKE . . ."

- A piece of *Now and Later* candy: At first it's really hard and you don't even know if it's worth it. But, as you work with it, it gets easier, smoother, and more enjoyable.
- A 1,000-piece puzzle. At first, it's just a bundled up mess that doesn't make sense, but as the pieces come together, the idea becomes clear.
- Swimming upriver.
- Just one more thing I have to do in order to graduate.
- Walking with my eyes closed.
- A superpower.
- Walking in high heels; elegant and attractive, but sometimes painful.
- Working with an annoying little brother. You want to love him but . . .
- Riding in a car with someone who is texting and driving.

Sharing the results of these questionnaires with the group will provoke a useful conversation that serves at least two important functions: it helps students acquire new ideas about learning from their classmates, and it positions the instructor as someone who is approachable and attuned to student needs. During the first few weeks of class, in small doses, you could return to the results of this questionnaire, taking time to discuss student perceptions, expectations for learning, and areas of anxiety.

There are still other ways to demonstrate a welcoming disposition toward diverse learners: holding some office hours online rather than in your office; developing a low-stakes method of correcting student error that rewards effort and doesn't embarrass students (in chapter 4 we will look more closely at strategies for error correction); developing positive facial expressions and verbal reactions that encourage participation and risk-taking.

Reflection

Think for a minute about the climate for learning in your classroom.

- How would students in your class describe your "disposition"?
- Are you approachable if a student has concerns?
- Do you actively monitor student anxiety levels and have some strategies for easing concerns?

The following case study gives you an opportunity to consider the importance of instructor disposition. What are the ways the instructor has raised some barriers to learning?

CASE STUDY 2.3: TIME FOR LUNCH

Students in Professor Rotter's German 105 class begin to gather their papers and put their books and belongings in their backpacks. It is the end of the third day of class, and they are starting to fall into a more familiar routine. Above the din of student chatter and scraping chairs, Professor Rotter calls, "Okay, don't forget your autobiography assignment is due on Monday. No late work accepted!"

As students file out of the room, chatting, Martin holds back until he is the last student in the room. Professor Rotter is stacking materials on the front table. As his stomach begins a low grumble, he thinks, "It is definitely time for lunch."

"Hi, professor," Martin begins cautiously. "I need to give you this."

Professor Rotter looks at Martin and then glances down through his bifocals at the document he has just been handed. "And what is this?" he asks, while simultaneously hoping the line at the bistro is not getting long yet.

"It's my letter from the disability office," Martin offers. "Thanks," and he turns to leave.

"Well, hold on just a minute while I take a look," Professor Rotter interjects.

After what feels like an eternity to Martin, Professor Rotter looks up over the top of his reading glasses. "I've had these letters before. You look fine to me. What's wrong with you? What disability am I supposed to be accommodating here? It doesn't say in the letter."

Martin flushes and feels a sudden urge to disappear. "Nothing is wrong. I just take a long time to read. I have a reading disability, and I need more time on tests and quizzes," he manages to say.

"I see. Well, I can tell you, you won't need extra time on my tests. Students in my classes have enough time. Why don't you try the tests without this additional time? We'll see how it goes and then we can talk about it. I really think you'll be fine."

"But professor. . . . I don't think that's going to work for me," Martin says hesitantly.

"Try it. And then we'll talk." Professor Rotter puts the letter in his class folder, turns, and walks briskly out of the room. "Again, this semester," Professor Rotter mutters to himself. "There's always something with these students," and his thoughts turn to the bistro. "Maybe a Reuben sandwich would be good today."

Reflection Questions

1. What barriers did Martin experience in this scenario?
2. How is this interaction with Professor Rotter likely to impact Martin's attitude and performance in class?
3. There are times when a professor may have a concern about the faculty notification letter that is provided by the disability resource office.

    a. How could Professor Rotter have responded differently with his concerns?

b. How would a different approach to his concerns potentially change the classroom climate for Martin?

UDI Resolution

If you have been teaching for a while, you have probably received a faculty accommodation letter from the disability resource office on your campus. If you are new to teaching, you can be sure this interaction regarding an accommodation request is in your future in the college classroom. You may not have given the importance of this conversation much thought. But for a student who is new to the process of requesting accommodations and talking about a disability, this conversation is very important to future interaction with you as instructor.

Two UDI principles closely relate to instructor disposition: the importance of creating a *welcoming classroom environment* and promoting *interaction and communication with students* (see Principles 8 and 9 in table 1.2). With these principles in mind, let's consider the clear barriers that emerge in this interaction between Professor Rotter and Martin.

One prominent barrier for Martin is Professor Rotter's understanding of disability that is firmly entrenched in a medical model of student deficits. In this view, a disability means something is wrong with the student; it is not an individual difference, not a predictable aspect of human diversity, but rather a shortcoming or weakness on the part of the student.

The fact that Professor Rotter can't see the disability magnifies his suspicion that this is a ruse on the part of the student to gain an unfair advantage in his class. Rather than understanding and anticipating student diversity, Professor Rotter has responded to Martin's confidential information and request with an undertone of hostility and doubt.

Another element of Professor Rotter's displeasure with Martin's accommodation request is the fact that the student's disability is not labeled in the letter from the disability resource office. Professor Rotter voices his concern to Martin, though the letter is produced by an office within the institution. Martin has not written the letter, and he does not control its content. This misplaced complaint merely adds anxiety and confusion to the conversation for Martin.

A final and significant barrier is raised when Professor Rotter suggests that Martin does not need the accommodations he has requested. After already being questioned about the validity of his disability and probed for confidential information, Martin is now placed in the confusing situation of being told to try the class tests without the extended test time he is eligible to receive.

The cumulative effect of these barriers for Martin is the antithesis of an inclusive classroom environment! For Martin, any anxiety about language learning or concerns about the impact of his reading disability are now likely to be magnified. From an equity perspective, Professor Rotter's tone and response raise challenging and, for some students, insurmountable barriers to language learning.

While the instructor is clearly the antagonist in this scenario, the barriers that are raised in this case are not unique to Professor Rotter. In student focus groups conducted by the authors, students with disabilities in language learning classes reported experiencing similar challenges and negative attitudes about accommodations from instructors at times. When these barriers occur, students indicated they are more likely to withdraw from the class rather than endure a hostile learning environment and often re-enroll in a future semester of the course with a different instructor.

While the negative tone and brusque student treatment is obvious in this scenario, some of the questions Professor Rotter raises are shared by many faculty, including instructors who are student centered and inclusive in other ways. For example, you may also have wondered why the letter from the disability resource office does not name the student's disability. Wouldn't this be valuable information to help you understand and teach the student?

At the college level, the specific disability label is considered confidential information. Remember from chapter 1 how different this is from high school special education supports that provide testing for students and grant specific services according to disability labels. And yet, the question of how to support individual student learning is a good one. When a student with a disability approaches you with the faculty notification letter, rather than ask about disability labels, have a conversation about learning. Encourage the student to come during office hours and talk about questions such as these:

- Tell me about your experiences with language learning in the past. What has worked well? What's been hard for you?
- How do you learn best in general?
- What strategies do you use for language learning?
- Is there anything else I should know that would help me support your learning in the class?

The focus of this conversation is on student learning. Individual strengths and weaknesses are framed as normal and expected. A tone is set for providing accommodations, but also being available to talk about learning challenges that may arise.

Another question raised by Professor Rotter pertains to encouraging a student to forego the use of accommodations such as extended test time. You may have wondered, is it ever appropriate to encourage a student to take the test without accommodations and "see how it goes"? This is not advised.

While your intent may be to challenge the student in a positive way, there is an undeniable power differential between student and faculty, making it very difficult for a student to speak up and insist on receiving accommodations. It can be interpreted as denying the student's legal rights, which, in a worst-case scenario, could lead to a discrimination complaint on campus or with the Federal Office for Civil Rights.

Consider as well, what if the student takes the test without accommodations and fails? Will you drop the grade? Will you allow the student to take a retest with more time? Will you insist the student "earned" that grade? There are really no good options if your hunch about the unneeded accommodation is wrong.

Provide the accommodation, and if the student decides your tests do not require additional time, let that be the student's choice. If you are concerned that the accommodation on the faculty notification letter will compromise an objective of your course, feel free to reach out to the disability resource office to discuss your concerns. Most faculty notification letters include office contact information specifically for this purpose.

SUMMARY

This chapter has covered the basic elements of classroom set-up to prepare for diverse learners. As designers of your class, strategies are provided for examining the physical environment of your classroom, the instructional materials you use, and the syllabus you develop. Instructor disposition and the important elements of creating a welcoming classroom environment are also discussed.

In chapter 3 we progress to the topic of instruction in the classroom. What instructional strategies should you use? What do you need to consider when teaching in the target language? How can group work be designed to include all students? Brief case studies will explore these topics and challenge you to apply UDI and your growing skills as an inclusive instructor.

Chapter 3

In the Classroom

While designing inclusive structures and materials before the semester begins sets the stage for a welcoming classroom, the instructional strategies you use during the term shape your interaction with students daily. Once the class is under way, your role in an inclusive classroom shifts from anticipating possible student diversity to being attuned to the actual students in your class in order to select instructional methods, monitor overall progress, and respond to individual learners.

This chapter begins with an overview of instructional strategies that students with and without disabilities report as being most helpful to world language learning. Three fundamental aspects of language instruction—use of the target language, group work, and homework—are explored in greater detail because they are an integral part of language learning and can at times be riddled with barriers for students with disabilities. Being aware of these barriers and prepared to modulate instruction in response to student needs are key components of an inclusive language classroom.

SELECTING INSTRUCTIONAL STRATEGIES

The instructor's design of teaching strategies and classroom practices forms the core of everyday learning in the course. While some academic disciplines rely on a "sage on the stage" approach of providing class lecture to transmit knowledge, the pedagogy of world language classrooms has a long tradition of using varied and multisensory approaches to promote student communication and learning. Among the many options and choices, which approaches best promote an inclusive classroom?

The authors have explored this question through several research projects that emphasize the perspectives of students with disabilities. Earlier chapters mentioned insights and findings from student focus groups and individual student interviews. To build on the findings of these projects, the authors conducted another study—this time a survey of over 500 beginning- and intermediate-level language learners with and without disabilities.

The survey presented 10 instructional practices and asked students to identify the instructional strategies that were important to them as world language learners. Which of these strategies were highly endorsed by all students and which strategies were perceived differently by students with and without disabilities?

The results were telling. Over 75% of *all* students identified the following instructional strategies as important or very important to language learning:

- The *use of visuals* in teaching a new concept. This includes such approaches as presenting pictures with new vocabulary, using published materials, and providing manipulatives such as stuffed animals or tableware to illustrate what is being learned.
- *Repetition* in the target language including, for example, repetition of oral questions, repetition of sounds, and repetition of grammar drills.
- *Learning memory strategies* including helpful mnemonics, such as rhymes and acronyms, and the use of flashcards.

In addition, over 75% of students with disabilities included these instructional practices as important to language learning:

- Time available for *one-to-one teaching* such as support during faculty office hours, individual tutoring, or interaction in the language lab.
- *Multimodal teaching* or including more than one way of experiencing and applying information. This typically involves a combination of varied visual, auditory, and kinesthetic approaches such as use of PowerPoint slides, group work, student engagement in pair work, or online activities.
- *Active project work* including journaling, role plays, interviewing, or making a commercial.

Over 50% of all students endorsed these strategies as useful approaches to learning:

- *Use of games*, such as conjugation competitions, scavenger hunts, or team exercises.
- *Multimedia and real-life artifacts* not specifically designed for world language learning such as films, YouTube, and music videos.
- Use of *humor* in the classroom.

The least popular instructional approach for both groups was use of rhymes and songs (e.g., songs for children or current pop music). This was rated as helpful by 30% of all students.

The list gives a variety of strategies to consider in your classes. Many of the techniques endorsed by students closely align with several of the UDI principles discussed throughout this book. For example, providing students *flexibility* in how they learn is reflected in use of visuals and multimodal presentation of materials. Thinking about *tolerance for error*, or where students may predictably have difficulty or need additional learning supports, comes into play with repetition in the target language and providing time for one-to-one student support.

With these techniques in mind, now consider how this applies to your own role as teacher and designer of your course.

Reflection

Take a minute to think about the instructional strategies you typically include in your course.

- Are you surprised by any of the strategies that were endorsed by *all* students? Which of these strategies do you use on a regular basis in your teaching?
- Students with disabilities also strongly endorse one-to-one teaching, multimodal teaching, and active project work as important to language learning. Why might these be helpful instructional elements for students with disabilities? How can you include them more seamlessly in your instruction?
- Which "student-endorsed" strategies can you include on a daily basis in your classroom?

TARGET LANGUAGE

No area of second-language learning is more fraught for college students than the quasi-immersion experience of the classroom. This anxiety is perhaps to be expected. While instruction that is conducted primarily in the target language provides maximum opportunity for comprehensible input, particularly in a class that meets only three or four hours a week, it also unavoidably creates barriers by making learning progress visible to peers while at the same time removing standard coping strategies available to students in their first language.

> **STUDENTS SAY**
>
> *Julie on class participation*: "I get very nervous when I have to speak in English in front of anyone so in Spanish it's a little more difficult because I'm not perfect at it."

Source: Scott, Hildebrandt, & Edwards, 2010

The ACTFL recommends that world language classrooms use the target language almost exclusively. The rule of thumb is that 90% of classroom activities, including student-to-instructor interaction and student-to-student interaction, should avoid the students' native language. When oral exams, student presentations, pair dialogues, and daily participation are combined, it is possible that up to 40% of a final course grade may be determined by activities that require students to participate actively and spontaneously in the second language.

Even if they might recognize the educational value of this practice, few students embrace it. In the authors' research interviewing students about their experiences with world language learning, the perception, even among confident students, is one of risk, uncertainty, and embarrassment. The boxes entitled Students Speak in this chapter include comments from some of the student research participants.

Interactive, extemporaneous activities, such as role plays, interviews, surveys, speed dating, mingling, games, and class-wide debates, introduce a certain levity to standard instruction and distinguish world language courses from most other classes encountered at the university. However, even these low-stakes exercises tend to produce high levels of anxiety for the language learner.

From the student perspective, a Spanish class conducted primarily in Spanish is akin to walking a tightrope without a safety net. Anyone teaching a second language has heard the standard student laments:

- "How am I supposed to learn the language if I can't comprehend what the instructor is saying?"
- "How can I ask a question if I can't speak English?"
- "We had to be fluent just to be in this class."

While the instructor understands that instruction in the target language does normally include a safety net, the task in the inclusive classroom is to help students identify the supports that will help manage anxiety and encourage participation. Some supports are more obvious than others. How many of the strategies in textbox 3.1 are you familiar with?

> **TEXTBOX 3.1   STRATEGIES FOR SUPPORTING USE OF THE TARGET LANGUAGE**
>
> 1. Provide a list of common classroom phrases that function as a script for students who seek help or need to ask questions.
> 2. Teach students to formulate questions in the target language and use circumlocution to reach for words they don't yet know.
> 3. Introduce the concept of metacognition and facilitate repeated conversations at the lower levels in the native language about why target language use is critical to learning.
> 4. Decode the textbook so students know where to find key information.
> 5. Use language in realistic scenarios and contexts.
> 6. Plan for predictable moments of respite from using the target language and structure manageable chunks of activity in class.

First, it is not unusual to provide a list of common classroom phrases that function as a script for students who seek help or need to ask questions. While lower-level classes might begin with basic questions such as "What page are we on?" or "How is that spelled?" higher-level courses will graduate to more open-ended inquiries. It is a common practice to review this list of expressions during the first week of the semester, but, since repetition is the heart of language learning and something valued by 75% of students, its effectiveness increases if it is reviewed regularly at various points throughout the sequence.

Second, at the intermediate level and beyond, it can be helpful to encourage students to formulate questions in the target language and use circumlocution to reach for words they don't yet know. How many times has a student disrupted the flow of a class conducted in the target language by saying: "I don't know how to say this in French, but . . ."? Students resort to the native language when they have genuine questions but haven't acquired the skills in the language to express their needs. Practicing question words and creating a climate that rewards constant use of the target language assist students in their climb toward proficiency.

Third, some student anxiety can be mitigated by introducing the concept of metacognition and facilitating repeated conversations at the lower levels in the native language about why target language use is critical to learning. Did you know that a study by Brown (2009) found that almost 40% of students have the misperception that they will be able to speak a second language fluently by the end of their second year of coursework? A conversation that debunks common myths and clarifies expectations might begin with the recognition that second-language study is slow going and sometimes infantilizing and can be enhanced by tips on how to study, especially when such skills are unique to the discipline.

Fourth, it is important to decode the textbook and class materials. Lower-level manuals typically include a large variety of stimulating units devoted to vocabulary, grammatical structures, cultural highlights, and readings, in addition to appendices and sections for review. Do students know how to distinguish vital areas from nonvital areas? Do they know which pages to review for a grammar quiz or which sections will help with a particular writing assignment? Is it obvious that they should look at the page of vocabulary while completing homework or participating in a conversation in class?

Fifth, to further support students in their development toward proficiency, model realistic uses of the language in the classroom. Basic instructions and commands, for instance, are easy to understand in the target language. Similarly, tasks that require students to produce language are more intuitive when they simulate real-life uses. Instead of asking students to create a dialog where they imagine meeting a celebrity at the bookstore, choose scenarios grounded in practical functions: calling to order a train ticket, giving directions to a campus visitor, describing a movie they would recommend.

One final technique for managing student anxiety, particularly at the lower levels, is to schedule predictable moments of respite when the native language is permissible. To use swimming lessons as a metaphor, think of this technique as training students to hold their breath for longer and longer periods of time. If pair work in the target language lasts for just 10 minutes at a time and is followed by 30 seconds of instruction in the native language before returning to the target language, students will understand that a "sink-or-swim" approach to world language learning is an outdated misperception.

Reflection

- How do you create a classroom environment that acknowledges both the need for almost constant input in the target language and a student's natural aversion to take risks?
- Think about your most successful classes in which students made clear progress in their speaking abilities. What went right?

CASE STUDY 3.1: THE SILENCE IS DEAFENING

Millie is majoring in global politics. She was advised in high school to enroll in American Sign Language (ASL) or Latin, both of which used English as the primary language of instruction. She selected ASL, which required no verbal output and very little written work.

In college, Millie's major requires her to learn a modern spoken language such as Arabic, Russian, or Spanish. The emphasis in these classes, as in her major, is on cross-cultural communication and understanding. With no previous background knowledge in learning a spoken language to activate, almost every part of her Spanish class is new to her.

While the teaching assistant (TA) for the class, Ana, has received a letter from the disability resource office and is aware that Millie is eligible for accommodations, she has noticed that Millie's accommodations are primarily supporting written assignments. Millie has requested and is receiving extended time to take tests and quizzes, as well as a peer notetaker for class. Ana is glad to provide these accommodations but finds it surprising that the spoken parts of the class—those proving especially challenging for Millie—are not addressed.

Millie is experiencing some surprises of her own. The mingling activities in class that require her to interview fellow students leave her feeling self-conscious and obtuse. When Ana introduces new material, Millie tries to ask questions when she is confused, but Ana keeps insisting she ask her question in Spanish. Asking Ana to repeat things multiple times is getting embarrassing. She dreads that feeling of her face getting flushed and that nervous giggle that bubbles up instead of her usual thoughtful responses. Once she finally understands the question, it takes her an inordinate amount of time to formulate a response and she is exhausted from the effort.

Ana is beginning to wonder how Millie will ever carry on a natural conversation with a native speaker and is concerned that Millie will struggle for semesters to come. She is also frustrated that the class's momentum seems to hit a snag whenever Millie attempts to answer a question. Ana has begun to consciously

> avoid calling on Millie because she worries Millie will either get embarrassed or bog down the class with her requests to repeat the question several times. Sensing Millie's frustration, Ana finds herself dreading the communicative activities that would otherwise seem like fun. An activity where partners compare the size of their families or plan a picnic takes twice as long as usual.
>
> The détente that Ana has settled on is unsatisfying. As a new instructor she is learning not to engage directly with the student, while the student, hoping not to make a mistake, is learning to say nothing at all.

Reflection Questions

1. Having recognized an impasse in her instruction, how should Ana start a conversation about this barrier? Should she approach Millie directly? Should she seek advice from fellow TAs or a supervisor?
2. Which strategies could Ana use to help all students, including Millie, feel more confident in speaking the target language?

UDI Resolution

As instructors who are fluent in the target language, perhaps even native speakers of the language, it is sometimes hard to relate to the struggles students may experience in this aspect of language learning. While many students experience anxiety interacting in the target language, the case of Millie and Ana explores additional barriers from both the student and the instructor perspectives.

Two UDI principles are particularly relevant in this case. Incorporating an instructional approach that includes *tolerance for error* and staying attuned to the *instructional climate* (see Principles 5 and 9 in table 1.2) are key considerations when promoting classroom interaction and use of the target language. In Millie's case, there is also reason to consider if there are barriers that require additional disability-based accommodations, but more on that follows.

When you apply these principles, one barrier for Millie is the fact that she has no prior experience learning a modern spoken language. Though there may be no prerequisite for registering for an entry-level Spanish course, in many college classrooms "beginning" language learners have completed one or even two years of high school language learning. While still at a beginning level by college standards, these students bring a basic vocabulary and experience using the target language.

Millie would have this same learning advantage if she were continuing her study of ASL in college, but as a new Spanish student, she is starting behind many of her peers. Consider also why Millie may have been advised to take ASL or Latin in high school. Students may choose these languages for many reasons. They are also sometimes recommended for students who have difficulty with spoken or written elements of language and language learning.

The strategies provided earlier in the discussion of target language are useful ones for Ana to incorporate into her teaching. For example, providing a list of common classroom phrases, encouraging and modeling circumlocution, or reminding all students to have textbooks open to topic-specific pages during conversations would give all students in the class, including Millie, a scaffold for target language use when needed.

Millie is also experiencing difficulty with the aural components of target language. While students do benefit from repetition and most students endorse this as helpful to language learning, Ana is struggling to balance what she perceives as the time-consuming needs of one student with the flow of the class.

One way to bolster Millie's ability to participate and reduce the in-class repetition is to post a list of topical questions the day before class. This support builds in time for Millie to process the questions and think about responses in the target language without requiring time in class. This strategy may benefit many new language learners as they build confidence and vocabulary in the target language. For instance, you may elect to add a column to your daily schedule to alert students to in-class expectations, such as "You will be prepared for class if you can describe members of your extended family, count up to 1,000, and use negative constructions without looking at the textbook."

So far this case has focused on strategies that Ana can use to anticipate challenges and support target language use. But perhaps the largest barrier, and one of the most challenging for new instructors, is the work of creating a classroom climate where students are comfortable taking risks with target language use.

Ana's own understanding of typical student progress in target language development is likely creating an inadvertent barrier. Her decision to stop including Millie in class conversation to avoid embarrassing her is understandable but not a long-term solution. Talking with the class beginning on the first day about the challenges of target language acquisition for all learners helps normalize the awkwardness and struggles in class. One of the reasons students learn a second language is to communicate with respect and cultural understanding. Modeling acceptance, humor, and support not only helps students develop essential language learning skills but also gives them the patience, tolerance, and acceptance to help each other along the way.

Ana may also be avoiding in-class conversation with Millie because she knows Millie has some form of disability. She may be struggling with trying to protect Millie's confidentiality in the public forum of the classroom. She may also be unsure whether it is appropriate to discuss a student's disability in areas beyond the formally approved accommodations.

Ana has made an astute observation that Millie's accommodations are somewhat limited in nature. They appear to focus on written assignments but do not address the barriers she has noticed for Millie in the aural/oral components of the class. It is entirely appropriate for Ana to invite Millie to come talk with her in the privacy of office hours to discuss how the class is going and how accommodations are working for her. Are there other ways to support Ana in class? Are there additional accommodations that may be useful?

Ana may also find it helpful to call the disability resource office to brainstorm other possible accommodations for Millie related to the unique demands of the world language classroom. It may be within Ana's purview to add additional accommodations, even if they are not indicted in the official materials from the relevant campus personnel.

GROUP WORK

World language classrooms are notoriously interactive. An hour in an intermediate-level German class, for example, with its role plays, storytelling, video clips, pronunciation drills, and organized play, mirrors to a degree the high-energy, imaginative atmosphere of a typical kindergarten. The same active process of language learning that students encountered in their first language does not change drastically as they learn their second or third, whether the student is 5 or 18 or 25 years old.

When proficiency in a new language is the goal, active engagement makes sense. To be a proficient swimmer, to return to the swimming analogy, you must first get wet. To learn the guitar, you must strum an instrument. To speak German, therefore, you must speak German. As much as learning requires the guidance of a competent teacher or coach, it also involves frequent practice to improve muscle memory, reaction times, or stamina.

To facilitate interactive learning, instructors of world languages are fortunate to be guided by the 2017 NCSSFL-ACTFL Can-Do Statements, the result of a collaboration between the National Council of State Supervisors for Languages (NCSSFL) and the ACTFL. The Can-Do Statements are organized according to the Interpretive, Interpersonal, and Presentational Modes of Communication as described in the *World-Readiness Standards for Learning Languages*:

- Interpretive communication: Learners understand, interpret, and analyze what is heard, read, or viewed on a variety of topics.

- Interpersonal communication: Learners interact and negotiate meaning in spoken, signed, or written conversations to share information, reactions, feelings, and opinions.
- Presentational communication: Learners present information, concepts, and ideas to inform, explain, persuade, and narrate on a variety of topics using appropriate media and adapting to various audiences of listeners, readers, or viewers.

What do the Can-Do Statements look like in a college classroom? While some minimal interpretive communication may be achieved between the student and the instructor alone, authentic communication will inevitably entail various kinds of group work or student-to-student interaction. In any given week at the university, students in a lower-level language class will practice interpersonal communication in a myriad of ways: talking to their colleagues using the target language, participating in a think/pair/share exercise, mingling among their classmates to conduct a survey, or playing a party game that requires asking questions, making guesses, and reacting to input from others.

A typical college-level language class might also include higher-order activities that facilitate presentational communication such as creative projects in which students develop a slide presentation, prepare a formal debate, write a dialog, produce a video interview, or demonstrate a cooking technique. Invariably, these presentational exercises will require students to work in teams of three or more.

As any language student will recognize immediately, practicing three different forms of communication simultaneously without recourse to a native language is a very tall order. Drawing on multiple formal linguistic skills at once, exercises that require personal interaction also activate informal social skills that may not be standard in other college classes: physical mobility, recognizable speech, an outgoing disposition, manners, spontaneity, a sympathetic ear, and an awareness of social conventions across different linguistic settings. There is certainly an aspect of improv in every world language class—almost as if the student must learn to swim and play the guitar at the same time.

Barriers, of course, are plentiful. Interpersonal and presentational communication—encountering any language in its natural habit—almost always entails a certain level of anxiety. Extemporaneous public speaking almost always produces some natural stage fright. Addressing a stranger in an unfamiliar setting can be taxing. Those who have not learned to control such anxiety in their native language may have, nonetheless, learned to avoid situations where it is likely to occur. Yet such coping skills to combat anxiety may not be available to students in the world language classroom. Indeed, social anxieties may be exacerbated when coping mechanisms are unavailable and none of the classroom partners are natural speakers.

Another barrier students may encounter during group work activities may involve the complexity of the exercise itself. As a simulation of authentic communication in a classroom where no one is fluent in the target language, group activities may often require a lengthy explanation to get off the ground. Instructors would be well served to model every activity carefully and build in time for students to first understand the parameters of the exercise before they are asked to execute it.

As the authors interviewed students in lower-level language classes, an additional stressor became clear: the constitution of the peer group. Given the differing ability levels and preparation of students, as well as social dynamics, the team students work with can affect their performance on any given activity. Therefore, instructor choice in the way groups are formed can have unintended consequences for student learning.

There is no right or wrong method of group formation; all have their own advantages and disadvantages, and several factors should be considered. For instance, many students enjoy choosing their own partners, but a student with a psychological disability may have trouble with this task and benefit from having a partner assigned (of course, that same student might benefit greatly from working with a partner with whom he or she already feels comfortable). Pairing students by ability can mean that certain groups require extra time or support but may give some students a needed opportunity to work through material themselves at their own pace and get extra support from the instructor.

Many teachers prefer to use a variety of methods of group formation so that students are constantly working with new partners of differing abilities. The nature of the activity itself may also affect how groups are formed; for a 5-minute warm-up it may be appropriate to let students work with those around them, but for a multiday-graded project, a more thoughtful grouping may benefit students. Instructors should, therefore, consider the nature of the activity as well as the needs of their particular students as they are planning how to form groups.

Instructors should also think carefully about how to grade group projects, when grades are to be assigned. Group grades can be a tremendous source of stress both to students who are concerned that another's lack of preparation will affect them negatively and to students who are anxious that their own abilities do not measure up to those of other group members. Basing a portion of the overall grade on an individual's performance or production can help to alleviate this concern, as students have control over part of their grade regardless of what their group members do.

This portion of the grade could be a participation/effort grade assigned by the professor or other group members, or it could be based on the individual's performance in a skit or presentation. It is impossible to entirely separate an individual's work from that of the group, and each individual should indeed take responsibility for the group's production as a whole, but the instructor should certainly consider how group projects can be graded fairly based on the differing abilities and personalities of each particular class.

Reflection

- How do you select partner and group activities for your students? Do you base your selection on the material to be addressed or the students in the classroom?
- Are students aware of the purpose of specific communicative activities?
- How do you modify textbook communicative exercises to fit your students' needs?

CASE STUDY 3.2: OUT OF SIGHT, OUT OF MIND

Professor DellaNeva is a seasoned veteran. Over the course of her 20 years in the classroom, she has learned to adapt to almost any student need. Her classes are popular; her sections fill up faster than those of her colleagues. More important, her students are well prepared to enroll in advanced-level courses and, indeed, many of them pursue a major or minor in Italian because of her instruction. She is a good recruiter, a student favorite, and an award-winning teacher. She gives frequent presentations at professional conferences and tries to incorporate up-to-date methods in her courses—even those she teaches semester after semester.

This term, on multiple occasions, she has been surprised to find a student in her class who appears to be encountering barriers in some of her "go to" class activities. The student, Alicia, has a vision impairment. Registered with the Office of Disability Resources, she is, in many ways, a model student. She is a strong advocate for her learning needs and approached Dr. DellaNeva during the first week of classes to discuss the impact of her disability in the class.

Alicia takes most of her written exams in a private setting with enlarged typeface. She has assistive technology in her dorm room that enlarges the print of textbooks and workbooks. She uses her cell phone in class to enlarge some exercises and photocopies, but she requests that all documents and quizzes distributed in class be enlarged when possible. She sits at the front of the class to be as close to the whiteboard as possible and participates fully in almost all activities.

Since Professor DellaNeva's instruction has been informed by universal design throughout her career, she has some experience modulating her teaching to match the needs of her students. She typically provides documents electronically but quickly learned how to enlarge documents on the copy machine when needed. She always printed quizzes in large font. Unexpectedly, however, it took her several weeks to understand how standard group work activities were creating barriers for Alicia.

In Professor DellaNeva's Italian classes, students often turn to one another to practice vocabulary and structures using a list of prompts, pictures, or diagrams. To accommodate Alicia, Professor DellaNeva always brought an enlarged copy of the worksheet so she could see the print and communicate with her partner.

Occasionally, Dr. DellaNeva extends this kind of conversation by asking students to mingle throughout the room to talk to more than just a single person. Imitating a cocktail party atmosphere, students might be asked to seek out others who are majoring in the same field, who share the same hobbies, or who have visited the same foreign countries. Even with an enlarged assignment sheet, this task is a little more challenging for Alicia than it is for other students. Eye contact and facial cues—key components of communication in a second language—are difficult for her to detect, and she doesn't readily perceive those around her as they try to get her attention. It's also difficult for her to write down information when she's not at her desk.

Another version of this networking group activity asks students to interview a series of partners by asking the same question and responding to the various answers supplied by a constantly changing partner. Rather than arm each student with a photocopy, Professor DellaNeva invites half the class to stand in a line facing the screen where she has posted a series of prompts. Partners are lined up in front of those asking the questions, unable to see the screen.

As pairs complete their mini-conversations, students facing the screen move aside to interact with a new partner. After a few interviews, students switch sides, allowing those who now see the screen to take the lead in the conversation. Alicia, of course, cannot see the screen and must always play the more difficult role of the interviewee, rather than the interviewer.

A final activity that Professor DellaNeva has struggled to adapt is a review drill that uses a website learning tool like Kahoot or Gimkit. This is a pace-changing, comprehension check that asks students to use their cell phones to play a competitive, timed, multiple-choice game. It is usually a crowd-pleasing review exercise that introduces teamwork, levity, and drama during the last 15 minutes of class. After a question or prompt is displayed on the screen, students work together to choose an answer and enter it on their phones. To select the correct answer, students must match a color or shape to the proper response.

Every few weeks, when Professor DellaNeva would say "Okay, it's time for Kahoot. Please take out your cell phones and think of a team name," she noticed that, instead of sharing the excitement of the rest of the class, Alicia opted to visit the restroom. The third time this happened, she realized that Alicia couldn't participate in this kind of activity because she couldn't read the prompts on the screen or see the possible answers on her phone. A chemistry-building activity that typically energizes the class and gets them cheering in Italian, instead, deflated and excluded this student.

Reflection Questions

1. In which ways does Professor DellaNeva consider the learning needs of her diverse students when she manages her classroom activities? In which ways does she fail to consider these needs?
2. Once she recognizes that some activities could hinder learning, what changes might she consider?

UDI Resolution

While the UDI framework prompts instructors to anticipate student diversity and be proactive in using inclusive strategies in the classroom, the changing composition of college student cohorts requires a constant monitoring on the part of the instructor. In the case of Professor DellaNeva, we see that even the most prepared and experienced teacher may still encounter unanticipated barriers for students in the design of class activities.

What are the barriers in this scenario? Certainly there are many positive components of this class. Professor DellaNeva is an engaged teacher who promotes a positive learning environment and is attuned to individual student performance. She is willing to accommodate students and modify elements of her class as an integral part of her work. Yet it is clear that group activities involving engagement with other students and a change of pace for student involvement have created some barriers related to visual perception.

Two UDI principles are closely interwoven in thinking about barriers and strategies in this case. Promoting a *community of learners* (see Principle 8 in table 1.2) and being attuned to the dynamics of interaction among students is essential to group work in the world language classroom. And while it is natural to think of influences on classroom interactions related to student personalities, academic preparation, and motivation, in this case with Alicia, the importance of providing information that is *perceptible* (see Principle 4 in table 1.2) comes to the fore.

Professor DellaNeva has observed barriers in three different types of group activities. Let's consider each of these activities in turn for possible modifications and strategies. In the first activity, class participation appears to go smoothly while students work with partners on vocabulary and structure practice. When the activity extends to mingling among the larger group of students, Professor DellaNeva has anticipated Alicia's need and provided her the worksheet in larger print.

But Professor DellaNeva has astutely observed that the act of initiating and reciprocating contact with other students is not working in an equitable way in this activity. Her hunch is that the social expectation of making eye contact and reading facial cues in this unstructured task is creating a barrier for Alicia. Are there structures she could implement that would lessen this barrier?

One strategy she might consider, for example, is having students mingle in smaller breakout groups rather than the whole class. Reducing the number of possible conversational partners may make this task less prohibitive for Alicia. Another possibility could be to alter the hypothetical setting of the activity from the informal mingling at a cocktail party to other scenarios with more social structure. For example, changing the task to reaching out to a stranger in a library or grocery store to pose questions could set the stage for verbal prompts such as "Excuse me. Can I ask you a question?" or "Pardon me. I see you are reading a book about . . . ." These verbal prompts may be more detectable for Alicia.

In the second activity that Professor DellaNeva is pondering, students are working in pairs participating in mini-conversations. One student faces a screen while viewing prompts to use for interviewing the partner. Professor DellaNeva has noticed this activity isn't accessible for Alicia. With the prompts only provided to students with average vision, Alicia is prevented from playing the role of the interviewer. Providing the interview prompts in another format, such as a printed copy in large print, will help Alicia; giving all students the option of reading the prompts from a printed copy or the screen may broaden access even further, giving students with reading disabilities or attention difficulties options for preferred format as well.

And the final group activity Professor DellaNeva is questioning is the popular and energizing online games that she uses with the class for an interactive comprehension check. We know from the previous group activities that information provided solely via screen excludes Alicia. By now, Professor DellaNeva is realizing that multiple formats, such as reading the screen aloud in this context, are needed in each of her group activities. The online games' heavy reliance on sight for team responses via phone is another perceptual barrier. Could students respond via iPad in order to benefit from a larger viewing screen? How will she address barriers for students with color vision deficiency (or color blindness) in detecting color-based responses?

While new apps and other technology-based learning opportunities can be fun and engaging, they do need to be reviewed through an inclusive lens.

- Is there flexibility in how the activity is perceived?
- Are there options for how students respond or engage with the activity?
- Are there ways the instructor can implement strategies to broaden access?

In some cases, the technology-based activity may not be accessible by all of your students. If that is the case, what is the message you send to the class if you use the technology anyway?

As an experienced instructor, Professor DellaNeva will be able to adeptly modify and tweak her instruction to remove many of the barriers inherent in her group activities. One more strategy to include is, of course, to reach out to Alicia directly. Inviting the student to come talk with you during office hours opens the door for learning about what's working, what other strategies may be useful, or even what other barriers may be latent in your group activities.

EFFECTIVE USE OF HOMEWORK

A final feature of inclusive pedagogy to consider concerns the daily assignments students use to prepare for each lesson. Frequently these assignments accompany the published textbook and are completed in a workbook or online. The method of assigning homework, as well as the schedule for completing it and the manner in which homework exercises are addressed in the face-to-face classroom, has ramifications for student engagement and learning.

Regular, predictable homework that allows students to practice new vocabulary, grammatical structures, listening techniques, and writing and reading strategies helps students manage the process of learning a language by isolating distinct linguistic elements. It reinforces the skills and concepts discussed in the classroom. In a perfect world, students use their executive functioning skills with homework assignments to test themselves, to enhance their understanding of general concepts and exceptions, to foreground their deficiencies, and to prepare for class. What barriers might be anticipated in the process of assigning, reviewing, collecting, and grading homework assignments?

As instructors develop a syllabus for the semester, they undoubtedly pair homework assignments with lessons that review older material or introduce something new. When classroom activities are designed to target a unit on family structures and the past tenses, for instance, instructors will assign homework that requires students to activate appropriate vocabulary and review appropriate grammar. Whether the homework is to be completed before or after the material is addressed in the classroom, instructors typically see a clear connection between the work a student does at home and the work performed in the classroom.

Do students see this connection? In the book *How Learning Works* (2010), Susan Ambrose and colleagues report that novice learners (those who are new to a topic) and expert learners have very different levels of understanding of how ideas and concepts are organized and relate to one another. Sharing the intended connections of homework and classroom activities helps students begin to see the relationship of ideas, or mental models, that are obvious to the instructor.

For example, from the instructor's point of view, homework is very tightly scripted, such that exercises completed outside class focus very specifically on a small portion of the target language that closely matches the activities in the classroom. Many published workbook activities also follow a well-organized, scaffolded structure in which students first complete simple discrimination activities, such as multiple-choice drills, before moving on to higher-order exercises such as open-ended exercises, reading passages, and mini compositions.

This progression, moving from simple to complex tasks, may not be obvious to students as novice learners. Helping students to be aware of this progression of levels of difficulty promotes their understanding of linguistic structures as well as giving them a framework for assessing their own performance. Knowing that classmates may be experiencing difficulty with certain parts of a homework assignment as well may bolster student confidence to ask questions.

Given these faculty expectations—that students will see a connection between the work they do at home and the way they perform in class and that students will understand their own deficiencies and use that understanding to improve—many publishers have moved homework exercises to online platforms. This development ostensibly benefits instructors (who no longer need to grade every assignment) and students (who can receive instantaneous feedback). At the same time, online homework exercises have some inherent challenges and can create barriers to learning.

Homework exercises may create barriers when instructors design the work completed at home to be distinct from the work completed in the classroom. While no instructor wants to use face-to-face contact time to review every homework exercise, students may come to class with questions that arise in the completion of their out-of-class assignments. Those questions might be usefully content based, such as when a student misunderstands a key grammatical element. These are important questions to address during class time and a prime opportunity to integrate homework with classroom activities. Allotting time to review or respond to homework questions at the beginning of each class session is an easy and predictable structure to implement.

STUDENTS SAY

Franklin on use of homework: "When the teacher actively looked at our homework and figured out where we had trouble and what we needed to work on and then put that up on the board or a PowerPoint or something, that helped."

Source: Scott, Hildebrandt, & Edwards, 2010

However, homework questions might also concern mechanics of an exercise itself, especially when directions are unclear or when an exercise lacks a model, addresses a rare exception to a grammatical rule, or is unusually complex. If these questions arise on a regular basis, this is a red flag for your instructional design because the well-intended homework assignment is instead building student frustration and taking time away from reviewing language concepts. If you are using a textbook's online homework for the first time, it is well worth the time to preview the assignments and provide an in-class preview of complex questions.

Assigning, scoring, and clarifying homework exercises can bring up a host of concerns about accessibility and inclusion. Some key questions to consider in this aspect of your instruction are highlighted in textbox 3.2. Each area is then discussed in more detail.

> **TEXTBOX 3.2 GUIDING QUESTIONS FOR MAKING HOMEWORK ASSIGNMENTS MORE INCLUSIVE**
>
> 1. How much homework is reasonable to help students integrate key concepts?
> 2. How often will exercises such as drills and rote memorization be collected, addressed or rewarded in the classroom?
> 3. Is the online platform for homework accessible for students who use screen readers?
> 4. How much trust will an instructor place in the automated grading provided in the online platform?

Is the online platform for homework accessible by students who use screen readers? Online homework platforms are typically provided directly from the publisher and are most often used by multiple faculty within a world language department. Ask your colleagues how they have addressed this previously. Consult with the disability resource office about how the materials can be made accessible.

How much homework is reasonable to help students integrate key concepts? How much is too much? Think carefully about why you have included homework as part of your instructional design. Talk with students in your class about how the workload is going.

How often will exercises such as drills and rote memorization be collected, addressed or rewarded in the classroom? Some faculty structure their class to collect all homework for a unit just before the test; others choose to assign and collect it more intermittently. Many students with disabilities experience difficulty with organization, planning, and time management. Consider collecting and reviewing homework more frequently with the class, particularly at the beginning of the semester while students are establishing learning routines.

How much trust will an instructor place in the automated grading? While there is an advantage to students receiving immediate feedback on their homework, there are times when the automated grading may be overly rigid. Remind students that you are available during office hours to discuss questions related to homework.

Reflection

- What is the goal in assigning homework to students? Do you assign homework so that students will learn basic material before coming to class? Do students use homework to review lessons from long ago or commit new material to memory?

- How do students learn of your approach to assigning homework and your expectations for completing it?
- How much homework do you review in class, and how do you know when that review is appropriate?
- What should a student do when he or she is genuinely stumped by a homework exercise, particularly one that is graded automatically online? Is it possible to foresee an exercise that will probably confuse students?

CASE STUDY 3.3: WHEN BEST-LAID PLANS GO AWRY

Thomas's face-to-face German class requires him to use an online workbook to complete homework assignments. The course syllabus clearly outlines which exercises are to be completed and states that students will be able to attempt each activity just two times before it is scored automatically. The TA instructor for the class, Lillian, asks that all published homework assignments be completed by the date of the unit test. While the student is encouraged to complete about seven exercises each night, they are not collected until the end of the chapter and they are not discussed regularly in class.

The online homework format has made learning difficult for Thomas. He was always very successful in language courses in high school. Some of the characteristics of his autism have been a good match for many aspects of language learning. He has a strong vocabulary in English and finds the similarities and differences with the German language fascinating. He is an expert in details and trivia related to World War I and frequently brings up little-known facts about German folk songs during class time.

Thomas's class performance has been strong, though at times Lillian finds he is a bit overbearing in class conversations. She is curious to see how he will do on the first unit test. As Lillian works through the stack of papers grading the newly completed tests, she comes to Thomas's exam. There is a note scrawled at the top:

Dear Professor: It was not possible to complete the unit homework last night. Your computer program is faulty. I could no longer continue when it insisted on marking items wrong that were obviously correct. I am sorry. I know you hoped it would be helpful, but it was not.

Sincerely,
Thomas

Reflection Questions

1. What barriers did Thomas experience with the online homework?
2. How should Lillian respond to Thomas's note?

UDI Reflection

Lillian is a new instructor, who is doing many things well in setting up her world language class. She has planned her course and provided students with a complete syllabus outlining class expectations. Homework is included as a regular part of class routines, and information is provided about due dates and grading. By assigning homework that is due before each unit test, Lillian is attempting to streamline her time demands and potentially give students additional flexibility for when to complete assignments over a four-week time period.

Given these well-laid plans, what are the barriers that Thomas has encountered? The UDI principles, *simple and intuitive* and *tolerance for error* (see Principles 3 and 5 in table 1.2), highlight the importance of carefully considering where students may experience difficulty with a learning task and using this insight to build in clarification, options, and scaffolds for student support.

Lillian has provided a schedule for completing homework that reveals some assumptions about her students. As an expert in language learning, she knows that regular practice outside of class is essential to acquiring language skills. Yet her homework structure conveys to students that doing the homework any time up until the unit test is acceptable.

Thomas has done what many students in the class are likely to do—complete work for other classes that have more immediate deadlines and then rush through the language homework at the last minute so he can receive full credit by submitting assignments before midnight on the last day of the chapter. Students in world language classes come from a variety of academic backgrounds. Beginning language learners, in particular, need to be introduced to effective learning routines and supported in developing study habits, including short and consistent practice outside of class.

You may be thinking to yourself, *but the point of homework is independent practice. Students need to just buckle down and do the work*. Many students in college need to develop more effective study habits, and some will develop these on their own. When you consider the diverse learners in your class, however, some students need more explicit support. There are some forms of disabilities, for example, that make these time management and executive functioning tasks particularly difficult. Students with ADHD and students on the autism spectrum such as Thomas often have difficulty with planning, organizing, and completing tasks. Assigning homework with more frequent due dates reduces the scale of this task and provides the opportunity for more frequent check-ins about student performance.

Another assumption embedded in Lillian's homework structure is that students will understand all of the concepts covered in class. Homework then becomes a matter of routine practice. By only collecting homework at the end of the unit, Lillian is missing out on important formative feedback about student learning in her class. Are there homework assignments that many students failed? These are topics that warrant additional instruction or support. Using homework as a "diagnostic" tool for instruction can give Lillian important feedback about her teaching and greater insight into the progress of diverse students in her class.

The automated grading system in the scenario presented another barrier for Thomas. While providing immediate feedback is a positive feature, the "two strikes and you're out" policy may be experienced as overly rigid and unfair by students. You might ask yourself whether this approach is supporting the inclusive classroom climate you have worked to engender with your class. How can you build in time and opportunities for a student who, for example, suspects that some of his or answers to open-ended questions might actually be valid, though not recognized by the online program?

The case with Thomas and Lillian highlights some of the dilemmas of using and assigning online homework in effective ways. Lillian's intention is to challenge her students by requiring homework practice outside of class and expecting that students do this independently. Yet the "challenge" for Thomas is one of time management, organization, and the ability to get clarification for errors and questions.

While Thomas's experience provides insight into some potential barriers in online homework, his experience is not unique. Think about the range of students in your world language classroom. How can you balance instruction that challenges them while keeping all students on board? Consider these strategies to help scaffold student learning outside the classroom:

- Begin the term with frequent homework due dates and checks-ins.
- Preview homework assignments to identify items that are complicated and may need clarification.
- Start each class session with homework highlights or time for questions.
- Explicitly remind students how homework supports effective language learning.

SUMMARY

This chapter examined core instructional strategies in world language classrooms. Beginning with an overview of methods that are favored by students with and without disabilities, the discussion shifted to frequently used teaching methods in world language classrooms. Strategies and discussion included ways to reexamine the fundamental language pedagogy of using the target language, group work, and homework in more inclusive ways.

In chapter 4, the focus of inclusive teaching turns to the important element of assessing student learning. What barriers do students experience in some of the most frequently used assessment techniques? How can you decrease student anxiety by making the assessment process more straightforward? Are there ways to increase student self-determination in the assessments you design? Case studies and discussion will continue to encourage your exploration in this important aspect of an inclusive classroom.

Chapter 4

Assessment of Student Learning

Assessing student learning is an integral part of language learning classrooms. It is an important means to measure the extent to which students are achieving the course objectives and learning outcomes you have carefully developed for your class. How you provide assessment and feedback to students, however, is much more than a grading opportunity, making the structure, frequency, and tone of assessment key considerations in an inclusive classroom.

This chapter provides a guide for reexamining your assessment practices. Are your assessment measures really targeting the skills and knowledge you intended, or are there latent barriers for some students? Does your feedback facilitate learning or increase anxiety? Are there ways you can more clearly convey your expectations to students while supporting student self-determination? Being attuned to each of these areas is integral to inclusive assessment practices in your classroom.

AN INCLUSIVE FRAMEWORK FOR ASSESSMENT

There are many resources related to using assessment techniques that are pedagogically sound in the world language classroom. Some basic concepts are important to reiterate here as a reminder before turning to a more focused look at inclusive strategies.

- There are two types of assessments: *formative*, which provide students with ongoing feedback on their achievement and seek to improve their performance, motivation, and self-assessment; and *summative*, which are used

to evaluate a particular student's achievement of learning outcomes and course objectives.
- It is important to align assessments with course objectives as you design your course. Ask yourself, *What do I want my students to know and be able to do as a result of instruction?* Assessment should then pertain to that particular skill or knowledge.
- Expectations for assessment should be laid out clearly at the beginning of the course, and guidelines should be made available to students in the syllabus and on the class website.
- Students should be tested in the same way they were taught; the test should measure the skills or knowledge targeted by the teacher, not each student's ability to navigate a new format or instructions presented in an unfamiliar way.

In addition to these foundational concepts, what else do inclusive instructors need to consider when assessing student learning? Martha Thurlow and her colleagues (2008) at the National Center on Educational Outcomes provide a helpful suggestion that instructors make a distinction between the knowledge, skills, and abilities you want to test, known as the *target skills*, and other non-construct information which may act as a barrier to students. They refer to the non-construct information as *access skills*.

To understand how target skills and access skills apply to written forms of assessment, consider this example. It is common practice in many world language classrooms to distribute a classroom quiz in hard copy format. The questions on the quiz comprise the target skills, but in this instance, the quiz also requires the access skill of being able to see the document. Obviously, visual acuity is not something the instructor is intentionally assessing. But written quizzes and tests can also contain more subtle access barriers. (See the discussion in chapter 2 on providing accessible instructional materials if you need a reminder on how to prevent this barrier.)

Now consider the same hard copy quiz with small or irregular font size, matching activities that are not visually aligned, questions added at the last minute in the instructor's handwriting, or exercises without directions. Not only does the document look haphazard and unprofessional, but it may be unreadable or unnecessarily complex for students who have difficulty with visual processing, attention, or working memory. This includes many students with LD or ADHD, for example. The performance of these students on the quiz will have little to do with their knowledge of the target skill the teacher is hoping to assess.

The following list of questions provides a guide for improving the accessibility of your tests and quizzes. Once you confirm the target skills you are assessing, look closely at your test for access assumptions you may have made.

- Is the visual layout of the test or quiz simple and easy to navigate? For longer tests, use headers to clearly distinguish different types of questions. Test sections should flow logically, and single sections should be kept on one page wherever possible.
- Is the font style and size easy to read and consistent throughout the document? Using larger font size and spacing between items will make the document easier to read for some students.
- Are the instructions precise and easy to understand? Consider the level of language learners in your class to decide whether directions will be provided in English or the target language. For more complex questions, include a model response to support student comprehension.
- Have you planned the test in accordance with how materials were presented in class and how other assessments were conducted in the past? If you provide a study guide to the class, has it included questions in a similar format? Remember the purpose of a test is rarely to assess the student's ability to understand novel directions.
- Have you included questions in a variety of formats (e.g., short answer, essay, multiple choice, true/false)? If so, are students prepared for this variety?
- Are you prepared to provide the test or quiz in electronic or other alternate formats?

Of course, assessment in world language classrooms is far from limited to written tests and quizzes. Most language learning classrooms already use a variety of means of assessment, including presentations, projects, portfolios, in-class participation, group work, and compositions. Just as using multiple methods of instruction allows students to learn in different ways, so using a variety of types of assessments allows students diverse ways of demonstrating knowledge.

Applying an inclusive lens to these varied assessment methods, are there ways you can introduce additional flexibility and choice into your assessment design? These important aspects of UDI are key elements for promoting student self-determination and engagement with language learning. This can be as simple as allowing students to choose the topic they develop for class presentations, or it can involve student input in a variety of other ways.

Anne-Marie Womack (2018), director of writing at Tulane University, suggests examining the disability-based accommodations that students have requested in your class in the past and focusing redesign efforts to increase flexibility for all students in those areas. For example, many disability-based accommodations relate to needing additional time. One strategy that builds in additional flexibility for all students is to include a "time bank" for assignments or projects; all students are given a two-day grace period for one assignment of their choice or two, one-day extensions for two different assignments.

Is it feasible to build in more flexibility with how you determine student grades in your class? With a clear understanding of course objectives and the target skills required, could students be allowed to weigh some assessments such as projects, tests, or compositions more heavily toward the final grade? Womack notes that instructors in a variety of academic disciplines use grade contracts such as this to involve students to at least some extent in how their grades will be determined.

Tammy Berberi, a professor of French at the University of Minnesota-Morris, develops grading rubrics in collaboration with students (more on grading rubrics in the following section). She works with students to identify up to five criteria for a given project, and they weight them together. A target skill that applies to all projects is quality of expression in French, which tends to be weighted at around 40% of the grade. To add further flexibility, Berberi notes, "When I know a student will have particular difficulty with one of the criterion, I allow every student to opt out of one of them" (personal communication, June 16, 2018).

Reflection

Take a minute to think about the different forms of assessments you use in your class. For each assessment (quiz, test, project, etc.) think about the target skills you are seeking to assess.

- What are some of the access skills you may inadvertently be assessing?
- How can you revise your assessments to eliminate possible barriers?
- What strategies can you incorporate to give all students more flexibility or choice?

CASE STUDY 4.1: WHAT AM I REALLY ASSESSING?

Federico had enjoyed the faculty learning community he had participated in last year. The Center for Teaching and Learning on campus had posted the opportunity online, and Federico was glad he had applied and been accepted. Six instructors on campus from different departments had met once a month to talk about Universal Design for Instruction (UDI) and inclusive teaching. In the process of being new to campus, getting oriented to the expectations of his tenure-track position, and teaching four classes each term, he hadn't realized how much he had missed having the opportunity to take time to reflect on his teaching and share some of the issues and ideas with peers.

Now it was August, and Federico was reexamining his syllabus and plans for Spanish 201. He hadn't taught the class since last fall, and he was curious about how much his perspective on inclusive teaching might have changed. As he looked over some of his previous tests and quizzes, he paused. He had relied heavily on traditional chapter tests to assess student learning.

"Hmmm," he thought to himself. "I have some work to do."

The following is one section of the test Federico is reviewing.

Section 1: Listening

I. **Comprensión auditiva.** *Escuche la conversación entre Pía y Mónica y después indique si las frases son ciertas o falsas. Si es falsa, re-escriba la frase correctamente.* (5 puntos)
1. Pía no cree que la democracia funcione. C F
2. Mónica no ha ido a votar porque no ha tenido tiempo. C F
3. Pía piensa que el candidato liberal es mejor que el conservador. C F
4. Mónica cree que no es importante informarse antes de votar. C F
5. Mónica finalmente decide ir a votar. C F

Reflection Questions

1. What are the target skills Federico is assessing?
2. What access skills are required in the test as it is currently written?
3. What barriers may be present for students?
4. What strategies or revisions does Federico need to incorporate to make this test more inclusive?

UDI Resolution

Oftentimes when designing a course, it seems that the most expedient approach to assessing student learning is to use the tests provided by the textbook publisher. While these ready-made tests focus on important target skills and are designed to use language, patterns, and exceptions that students have recently studied, an inclusive instructor will look closely for access skills that may create barriers for the students he or she teaches.

In the test section that Federico is reviewing, the target skill, or the knowledge tested, is rather limited: whether a student can gather specific information from listening to a conversation between native speakers. The access skills and potential barriers embedded in the exercise, however, are multiple. Does the student have the ability to

- see the test questions?
- understand and follow multistep directions? and
- write or type the statements that are false?

Multiple UDI principles provide relevant guidance in this case. At a fundamental level, students obviously need to "see" or perceive the test (see Principle 4 in table 1.2). When a written test question is provided in an accessible format as we have discussed throughout this book, the potential barrier is prevented.

The second access skill, understanding and following multistep directions, requires the instructor to consider whether the directions are simple and straightforward (see Principle 3). In this case, providing directions in the target language for a Spanish 201 class is likely an integral part of the target skills being tested. It is likely that students have completed homework assignments prior to the test that mirror this activity. However, if the test format of listening and responding to written questions is unfamiliar to students, it is useful to provide a model or sample response.

The speed of reading and processing of information will vary widely among your students. Sufficient time should be given for all students to become familiar with the true/false statements themselves. An approach that provides additional time for all students would be to give the statements in advance, so that on the day of the assessment students will already be familiar with them and can concentrate on the target skill of listening to the conversation. At the very least, the instructor could read through the statements aloud so that students understand what information they are listening for.

There are other ways to make a listening activity more accessible to all students and particularly to those who may have difficulty with listening comprehension. When it is possible, showing a videotape of the conversation will greatly aid students who are primarily visual learners. This is also a closer approximation of many real-life situations in which they might encounter the target language. A pre-listening warm-up—providing background information such as the identity of Pía and Mónica as college students who are having lunch together, and the fact that it is election day, and then asking students to think about what Pía and Mónica might be discussing—is another key strategy, particularly if this is a practice commonly used during listening exercises in class.

A final access skill embedded in the test question is the requirement for students to rewrite false statements. What, specifically, is accomplished by making students rewrite entire sentences, and would changing the requirements of the exercise lessen its validity? If not, the instructor may choose to change the instructions so that the student merely needs to circle the part of the sentence that makes it false or provide short answers rather than complete sentences.

ERROR CORRECTION

Given the diversity of learning characteristics and the variability of student preparation and performance, the topic of error correction is complex and multifaceted, although the questions it raises may appear simple at first glance:

- *How often should errors be addressed?*
- *Which ones should be corrected?*
- *What method of correction is most effective, realistic, or encouraging?*
- *Is indirect feedback more beneficial to the student than direct feedback?*
- *Who should do the correcting: the student, a peer, or the instructor?*
- *Should the method or frequency of correction change with the students' proficiency level, anxiety level, or learning profile?*

Multiple studies have attempted to answer these questions, with sometimes conflicting results. Two relevant points are, nonetheless, widely accepted: first, that tolerating *some* error helps to foster confidence in students and, second, that periodic and systematic feedback helps students progress toward proficiency.

In the communicative classroom, students are trained to use the target language through meaning-focused interaction rather than rote memorization or form-focused grammar practice. As discussed in chapter 3, much class time is spent on conversational practice. Corrective feedback during practice activities helps students recognize and fix their errors, leading to increased accuracy. However, while your preferences and methods, whether consciously considered or not, will determine the amount, type, and frequency of feedback, it is important to consider the barriers that may prevent some students from receiving optimal benefit from corrective feedback.

Instructors often provide feedback on students' verbal work through nonverbal means; raised eyebrows, a shake of the head, or a slight lean forward can draw a student's attention to an error. While these exchanges are typically immediate and informal, they can still present a barrier to students whose disability interferes with vision, in general, with reading body language, or with comprehending and responding to social cues. You can support these students simply by gaining an awareness of their own methods of nonverbal communication, paying careful attention during exchanges with them, and making nonverbal cues more explicit when it seems that a student is not responding to implicit signals.

Overall faculty disposition is a key factor that may change how a student responds to error correction and determine its effectiveness. Students must feel comfortable participating, taking risks, and making errors. For students to receive and internalize error correction, especially on an ongoing basis, they need to feel that you personally believe that they are capable of learning the language. Cultivating attitudes of approachability and responsiveness to individual students' learning needs remains an important task for the language instructor seeking to support all students.

STUDENTS SAY

Monique on faculty error correction: "It's really important not to intimidate a newcomer."

Source: Scott, Hildebrandt, & Edwards, 2010

In addition to promoting an atmosphere of positive encouragement in the classroom, setting very clear standards for oral work and providing many low-pressure opportunities for practice are all steps that can help to mitigate anxiety barriers. Though tolerating some error in speech can help students gain confidence, instructors must strike a balance between this and helping students to improve their grammatical accuracy through feedback. You must also be aware of students' varying levels of sensitivity toward being corrected in front of others. Errors should be corrected in a nonjudgmental way at all times.

While oral assignments and in-class participation call to mind barriers related to classroom atmosphere, communication skills, and faculty characteristics, written assignments often present barriers for students whose disabilities affect visual processing and interpretation. In contrast to verbal feedback and correction, which are typically immediate and informal, written error correction comprises part of a process that is frequently used as a summative assessment. Some of the principles for designing inclusive assessment can also be applied to the writing process, in general, and the editing phase, in particular.

First, it is important to set very clear expectations as to what is required for the final product and what skills will and will not be assessed in the written product. Thresholds will differ for formative and summative assessments. These thresholds should be clear to students. Many instructors are quite tolerant of error in verbal work, encouraging a student to take risks and say as much as he or she possibly can, only to take out the red pen and circle almost every word in the same student's composition or homework exercise. To establish clear expectations, you should correct only the errors in the material being assessed on the current assignment.

Second, as with other documents, any rubrics, guidelines, or explanations of the system being implemented to mark errors and correct edited drafts should be organized, neat, and legible. Standard proofreading symbols are sometimes used to mark students' drafts, while you may have your own written or symbolic systems; these need to be clearly explained to students.

There are many kinds of feedback that instructors may offer on written work: direct (correcting the errors), indirect (marking them with a code that signals to the student what to correct, as in writing "Sp." under a spelling error), or simply circling the errors and letting the student determine how to correct them. Unless individual, detailed guidance is an option, the latter two methods may present barriers to some students.

Students with disabilities that affect spelling or syntax may have great difficulty in identifying the nature of the error and correcting it. One study on written corrective feedback in beginning German classes showed that while different feedback types all lead to improved accuracy, direct feedback results in the greatest accuracy (Vyatkina, 2010). Providing direct, explicit feedback is one way to support students with learning disabilities on their writing assignments.

Finally, no discussion of error correction would be complete without mentioning the subject of peer editing, a fairly common practice in language classes. As with any group work, peer editing can be a barrier or a support to students with disabilities. Some students may feel a lowered sense of pressure when a classmate rather than a teacher is doing the editing and may enjoy and appreciate the input from peers.

Conversely, others may feel discomfort when a peer they don't know well is critiquing their paper or feel anxiety about their own ability to offer suggestions to a classmate. Similarly, a student with a disability that affects reading or visual processing may have significant difficulty identifying errors in another's composition.

> **STUDENTS SAY**
>
> *Eric on providing peer feedback:* "If you're struggling, you don't want to bring everyone else down."

Source: Scott, Hildebrandt, & Edwards, 2010

There are many ways of making the peer editing process more inclusive; one is simply to be available for one-on-one guidance for students who need help in identifying errors. One possible way to lower the social anxiety barrier is to let students have some input in the process of choosing their partners. Another is to have multiple students edit each paper and allow both the drafts and the editing and commentaries to be anonymous. Of course, allowing individuals the option to correct their own papers instead of another student's is an easy solution that may be more beneficial to some. While the efficacy of peer editing is debated by teachers, multiple studies have shown that guided self-editing leads to superior writing products.

Reflection

Think for a minute about our own strategies for error correction.

- Do you approach error correction in a systematic fashion, or does your feedback to students change with the assignment, your mood, your grading load, the classroom climate, or student engagement?
- Do students know what kind of feedback to expect when they turn in an assignment, complete a high-stakes test, write a composition, or participate in class activities? Where do you establish these expectations—On the syllabus? On the assignment itself? Verbally in class? As you are grading?
- When students work on peer editing assignments, how do you evaluate the quality of the student editor's work? How do you guide the editors as they evaluate a piece of writing?

> **CASE STUDY 4.2: THE ENTHUSIASTICALLY INCORRECT VOLUNTEER**
>
> Dr. Kim teaches a fourth-semester Korean course, the last in the sequence required for all students. His section includes a range of learners, but most are able to speak, read, and write

at the intermediate-low level. One student, however, Destanie, lags behind the others in the area of spoken production. During the first weeks of the semester, Dr. Kim could not understand how a student at this level could still pronounce words so incorrectly.

At first, he would correct her pronunciation every time she volunteered a response in class. While her answer was usually grammatically correct, he felt it would be impossible for a native speaker to understand what she was saying. Moreover, he assumed she should have learned basic pronunciation long ago and wondered why she seemed so headstrong in her demeanor. She insisted on speaking frequently in class but always gave answers in such an incomprehensible accent that it affected genuine communication.

Just before the first chapter test, Destanie presented a faculty notification letter from the disability resource office that specified that she would need extended time and unlimited attempts at the listening section of the assessment. While the student did not disclose the nature of her disability, Dr. Kim wondered if these accommodations had something to do with her verbal production and her perceived disposition in class.

Reflection Questions

1. How soon and in what manner should Dr. Kim approach Destanie about her performance in class?
2. When considering how to correct Destanie in class, how should Dr. Kim strike a balance between the needs of the individual student who may need support in communicating verbally and the needs of other students who will need to hear comprehensible input?

UDI Resolution

There are many facets of error correction in the language classroom. How do you gauge the level of correction and feedback that supports individual learning and progress? When the target skill being taught or practiced involves multiple students or even the entire class, such as in this case with Destanie, how do you balance the needs of one student with the needs of the broader classroom community?

Several of the UDI principles are instructive in this case. Dr. Kim has recognized a pattern of the difficulties that Destanie is experiencing in class participation. He has experimented to some extent with the level of error correction provided, first correcting every error and then backing off as this approach did not appear to be improving Destanie's performance. In thinking about other approaches to address these error patterns (see Principle 5 in table 1.2), what additional resources or supports might be beneficial for Destanie?

The best source of information is, of course, talking with Destanie herself. If Dr. Kim has already set the stage for open communication by including a disability statement in his syllabus and inviting students to contact him with questions during office hours, it is advisable to reach out to Destanie within the first three weeks of class. This should be done either directly through e-mail or discretely after class. The intent of such a meeting is not to ask whether Destanie has a disability. Rather, it is to share the observation that her written performance is stronger than her conversation skills and to talk further about how she has learned best in previous Korean coursework.

Often, when a conversation is focused on individual learning, a student may feel more comfortable disclosing a disability. Consider in this case that Destanie now mentions to Dr. Kim that she has a hearing impairment and wears hearing aids. She explains that this has little impact in most of her coursework, but she does need some accommodations, particularly with auditory components of tests. She also shares that it helps when an instructor faces her when speaking.

Reflecting on past learning experiences in Korean courses, Destanie notes she has not used any supports specific to pronunciation, but a previous instructor had told her that the more she practiced speaking and participating in class the more she would improve. Destanie explains she is working hard to be actively engaged in class.

Dr. Kim now has some helpful context for the verbal performance and class dynamics he has observed. He can refer Destanie to resources on campus that will provide additional opportunities for verbal practice and feedback such as a language lab, a graduate student mentor, an informal language lunch group, or a language learning community in the residence halls, for example. Dr. Kim can acknowledge Destanie's strong class participation effort but mention that there may be times when he cannot call on Destanie so other students have opportunity to practice their verbal skills as well (see Principle 8 in table 1.2).

Dr. Kim also now realizes that Destanie may not be accurately hearing the questions he poses or the responses of her classmates. He can easily rearrange the classroom desks to form a circle, so all students are facing each other during class conversation. Dr. Kim also makes a note to himself to face the class when speaking, making sure these important classroom conversations are perceptible (see Principle 4 in table 1.2).

With additional resources available to support Destanie's verbal practice, and a classroom environment that is arranged and structured in a more inclusive manner, Dr. Kim has eliminated some of the barriers to Destanie's language learning. While his goal is still for her to be understood by a native speaker, a threshold that is a common benchmark at the intermediate level, this may or may not be achieved. But with open lines of communication with Destanie, Dr. Kim can continue to give her corrective feedback and talk with her about her progress in this challenging area.

RUBRICS

In many ways, scoring rubrics in the world language classroom are the most inclusive of all documents. Their very purpose mirrors the principles of UDI: they demystify assessments and relieve anxiety by clearly communicating expectations about quality; they anticipate learners' questions; they concretize subjective criteria in an effort to make them predictable and consistent; and they serve as a tool for self-assessment and metacognition.

Many of the reminders in the sections in chapter 2 devoted to accessible documents and thoughtful design are applicable in this section on developing inclusive scoring rubrics. Like a course syllabus or class schedule, rubrics should be visually uniform, concise and clear, and easy to read and comprehend. A rubric that is presented at the moment an activity is assigned—whether the activity is a composition, a group project, or an oral interview—answers questions before they are asked and allows the student to budget energies in the most successful ways.

Consider the sample rubric in table 4.1 that helps students know what to expect during an oral assessment toward the end of the semester. The exercise (a conversation with a partner) is described in the target language, while the grading rubric is clearly outlined in the students' first language. The rubric follows a consistent format from earlier assessments and indicates the level of performance required for an average grade, and above-average grade, and an exceptional grade.

While the parameters of the activity are fairly open ended and allow for considerable creativity, the rubric directs the student to focus on the most important parts of the exercise: comprehensibility, use of appropriate vocabulary from the chapter, and strategies for communication. Success in these areas is described briefly so students are aware of how they can meet expectations, exceed expectations, or fail to meet expectations.

Table 4.1. Sample Grading Rubric for an Oral Activity

	Emerging: 0–1	Meets Expectations: 2–3	Exceeds: 4–5
Comprehensibility: how well are you understood?	Understood by teacher but with difficulty	Understood by native speakers who teach Spanish	Understood by any native speaker of Spanish
Vocabulary use: how extensive and applicable is your vocabulary use?	Uses basic vocabulary appropriate to the situation	Attempts to use a wide variety of appropriate vocabulary	Uses a wide variety of vocabulary accurately
Communication strategy: how well do you maintain communication?	Two communication strategies used; a few words in English	Several communication strategies used; no English used	A wide variety of communication strategies used; no English used

Source: Hildebrandt, 2010

Directions: You and your partner will present an interview with a celebrity. One person will play the role of an actor or musician; the other will interview him or her in a formal setting. You will discuss the arts, the work life, and the personal life of the celebrity using the vocabulary of the chapter. You will have 15 minutes to prepare the interview, which will last about 3–4 minutes.

The instructor will use the following rubric to evaluate your portion of the conversation.

Using this rubric to sketch out their conversation, students are aware of what is important in this particular context. Rather than race to a dictionary app to find an unfamiliar word, they will focus instead on the vocabulary in chapter 13, structuring an interview around words they do know. This rubric makes clear that the conversation, while fanciful, is guided by practical concerns: rehearsing new vocabulary about movies, theater, and music.

The rubric also emphasizes an ongoing concern about communication strategies and implicitly reinforces the goals of the course: to acquire the multiple skills needed to interact with someone in a second language. Presumably, the class has discussed communication strategies on a frequent basis. Such strategies may include introducing oneself and using an appropriate form of address, asking questions or reformulating a question that is not readily understood, using circumlocution to describe a concept or unknown word in a round-about way, or employing comparisons to get a meaning across. In a readily accessible way, this rubric reminds students to activate those familiar strategies as they encounter this unfamiliar setting.

Is it possible to make a scoring rubric flexible while also establishing uniform expectations? When instructors allow students to modify rubrics in order to highlight their strengths and lessen the impact of their weaknesses, it imbues the entire class with an inclusive ethos in which communication about learning and pedagogy is foregrounded and in which students reflect on their needs and abilities, advocate for themselves, and enhance their commitment to language learning.

The rubric in table 4.2 illustrates a different application of rubrics. You will notice that the instructor provides a range of possible weights for each element of the class that will comprise a student's final grade. Some choices important to the instructor have, nonetheless, been predetermined. For example, chapter exams will be the important summative assessment of the semester. However, depending on student choice, these high-stakes tests could count for as much as one-third of the overall course grade or as little as one-fifth. Students who typically perform well in oral interviews and spontaneous conversation may elect to count a cumulative spoken assignment as heavily as those chapter exams, while de-emphasizing the weight of written compositions. A student who usually writes well but is concerned about spontaneity would reverse those weights.

While the combined components of the rubric capture the learning outcomes of the course, each has been designated as either a formative assessment or a summative assessment. When the instructor reviews the syllabus at the beginning of the semester, this breakdown will naturally provoke a conversation about how language learning works. The formative assignments, such as daily attendance and regular homework, reward

Table 4.2. Sample Rubric for Final Grades That Incorporates Student Choice

The student's course grade will be determined by the following percentages:

Formative assessments	
(work that helps you learn)	
Attendance and contribution	10–15%
Online homework	10–20%
Vocabulary quizzes	5–15%
Summative assessments	
(work that shows what you know)	
Compositions	5–20%
Chapter exams	20–35%
Oral exam	5–20%
Final written exam	10–20%

students for effort and discipline and typically enjoy a higher level of tolerance for error. The summative assessments—the final exam and formal compositions—allow students to show the skills they have mastered. They have a lower threshold for error. Since students are able to distribute weights individually, they can choose which type of assessment is more useful to them.

The instructor may choose to permit variations in all areas of the class or may elect to allow students to adjust only certain areas. For example, perhaps you determine that completion of daily homework, as a highly controllable and highly formative element, is vital to success in the class and must account for the same weight for all students. In the example in table 4.2, it is clear that 65% of the overall grade is already accounted for (no component can be reduced below 5%) and that students are able to shift the weights of 35% of the total grade.

How does an instructor manage and track this kind of variability? One approach is to ask students to determine their weights during the first few weeks of the semester, after a series of conversations about learning needs, course expectations, and workload. At the end of the second week, for instance, students would sign a contract that fixes the weights of the components for the term. This contract would then be used by the instructor at the end of the term to calculate the overall course grade. Another approach is to allow students to adjust the weights halfway through the course, when they have more information about their performance in various areas.

Since communication is a key outcome of the course, as is metacognitive understanding of the process of language learning, a flexible rubric allows students to emphasize either written or spoken communication more heavily. A student with dyslexia, for instance, may wish to weigh the course more strongly toward spoken production, whereas a student with an anxiety disorder might privilege written communication. While all elements will carry some weight for all students, permitting students to manage the importance of various modes of communication may allow them to play to their strengths and indeed will mirror real-world application of the language.

Reflection

Think for a moment about possible applications of rubrics in your classroom.

- How does a grading rubric enhance an assignment for students with disabilities? What messages do you convey when you explain in detail how a student will be evaluated?
- How does a grading rubric streamline the grading process for instructors?

> ### CASE STUDY 4.3: HOW DO YOU SPELL EQUITY?
>
> Professor Kreuger has been teaching French to college students for five years. Even in that short period of time, she has noticed trends in spelling that have caused her to reevaluate the way she teaches writing. Text messaging and Twitter have de-emphasized the need for accurate spelling in her students' native language, and the prevalence of auto-correct software (in both French and English) has allowed students to approximate the spelling of unfamiliar or troublesome words anytime they use a keyboard.
>
> In a language acquisition course, though, where missing letters or accent marks can affect meaning and communication, Professor Kreuger typically conveys the importance of correct spelling. If students are asked to compose an e-mail, for instance, accent marks, verb endings, and adjective agreements will all come into play. Even in an informal spoken assignment, correct spelling might determine pronunciation or verb tenses.
>
> Just as Professor Kreuger was designing a rubric for a composition assignment early in the semester, she met with her student Trevon to talk about his dyslexia diagnosis and his history of difficulty with French. After their conversation, she started to reflect on ways to balance Trevon's abilities with the outcomes of the course. She was positive Trevon could demonstrate proficiency in French in multiple ways but was unsure how to design and score a writing assignment that could accommodate his learning profile.

Reflection Questions

1. How do you determine which elements of an assignment or an overall course are absolutely essential and which depend on a certain context? How do you inform students when you make such a determination?
2. How much do you consider a student's educational history and experiences when you assess their work?
3. Is it appropriate sometimes to evaluate students with differing criteria?

UDI Resolution

This scenario provides a good example of how students with disabilities or other diverse learners sometimes make an instructor look at what he or she is teaching and assessing in new ways. There is certainly long-standing practice in language learning classrooms to teach and assess written components of language, including accurate spelling. How can Professor Kreuger reconcile this practice with her observation that Trevon has other aptitudes that she can tap into in his work to become more proficient in French?

It is important to keep in mind that some students with learning disabilities such as Trevon have experienced extensive difficulty with spelling throughout their lives. You may observe that, despite high verbal aptitude, some students manifest unusual and inconsistent spelling patterns even in English and perhaps in spite of years of intensive support and compensation work prior to college. In an intriguing participant research study conducted by Charlann Simon (2000), she describes the process of her own professional and personal world language learning as a speech pathologist with dyslexia. She poignantly notes that "language learning is not a natural process for some of us."

One approach for working with Trevon is to consider his spelling difficulties as an aspect of his disability. In this scenario, Dr. Kreuger could talk with Trevon about accommodations he likely used in high school for language learning. A consultation with the campus disability resource office may also generate other suggestions for circumventing these difficulties through testing or project-related accommodations that would support Trevon.

From an instructional design perspective, however, how might Professor Kreuger use the conversation with Trevon to reexamine how she develops the rubric for the class composition assignment? The UDI principle of equitable use (see Principle 1 in table 1.2) suggests an approach of searching for an inclusive solution that is available to all students in the class.

Consider the contents of Professor Kreuger's current draft of the grading rubric. She is planning to base composition grades on five elements: organization, use of relevant vocabulary, use of relevant grammatical structures, use of relevant spelling and accent marks, and the integration of relevant cultural topics discussed in class. Rather than change her criteria, she elects to incorporate flexibility and equity for all students (see Principle 2 in table 1.2) by allowing each student to drop one of these criteria from the composition grading process. Trevon can now highlight the strengths of his composition while other students are given the same opportunity.

The Virtual Assessment Center at the Center for Advanced Research on Language Acquisition (CARLA) includes several resources to consult on this topic: http://www.carla.umn.edu/assessment/VAC/index.html

STUDENT SELF-ASSESSMENT

Throughout this book there have been suggestions and strategies for promoting student metacognition, that important step of making thinking processes explicit and supporting students in monitoring their own learning. While all students benefit from this support in "learning how to learn," some students with learning disabilities or difficulty in executive functioning find these strategies particularly valuable. The area of assessment offers additional opportunities to support metacognition.

The old axiom "learn from your mistakes" is a central feature of self-assessment activities. While students often view tests as strictly a task that results in a grade, there is an opportunity to help students to gain insight into their language learning by reflecting on test performance. This formative assessment opportunity is one in which students can use their experience to gain insight into their content knowledge, study strategies, and test-taking skills. Most importantly, students can use this information to inform how they prepare for and perform on the next test. While students may be highly motivated to improve class grades, this instructional tool ultimately enhances their overall approach to language learning.

Marsha Lovett and her colleagues at Carnegie Melon (2013) created a method called "exam wrappers." Typically, this is a brief set of questions that are attached to a test when it is returned to students. The questions can be adapted to your class and focus on the metacognitive skills you want to promote. Wrappers typically include questions in three broad areas:

- How did you prepare for the test?
- What types of errors did you make on the test?
- How do you need to change study habits and preparation for next time?

Applying this to world language classrooms, ask students to reflect on specific aspects of the test. For example, did the students' errors relate to specific types of questions (e.g., listening with a written response, vocabulary items, or conjugations)? Were errors related to test-taking skills (e.g., misreading directions)? Distinguishing the types of errors helps students to identify more useful goals related to language learning.

Students can complete the questions in class as a brief activity or for homework. It is useful to allow some class time for students to discuss their responses as well as share study and test-taking strategies. The wrappers should be collected by the instructor to monitor completion and can be graded or not. When it is time for students to start to study for the next test, the wrappers should be returned to students to remind them to use their new insights in preparing for the test.

The wrappers promote a deeper processing of the test content by students. They can also give the instructor greater insight into where students are having difficulty and where to target additional clarification or instruction. The wrappers method can also be used for projects or assignments where students would benefit from more reflection on the learning process.

Another prime opportunity for promoting student self-assessment is in the area of class participation. It is common practice to include class participation as part of the course grade. Giving students a daily or weekly grade in this area reflects the importance of verbal practice in language learning. But do students know what comprises "good" class participation? Is it enough to answer one question posed by the instructor? Is it good participation if a student is active in a group activity?

One way to make your expectations explicit and promote student awareness in this area is to provide a self-assessment rating scale. The example provided in textbox 4.1 is easy to use or adapt for your classroom. This tool is particularly valuable with beginning language learners to give them concrete actions that will help them monitor their performance. Students may be asked to complete the self-assessment more frequently at the beginning of a course and less often as they develop good participation habits over time.

TEXTBOX 4.1   CLASS PARTICIPATION SELF-ASSESSMENT RUBRIC

Directions: Rate yourself on these components of class participation. The highest possible point value is in parenthesis for each item.

1. I came to class on time with my homework completed. (+2 points)
2. I spoke only French to the professor. (+2 points)
3. During peer activities, I used English. (−6 points; no partial credit)
4. I asked a question in French. (+4 points)
5. I was prepared enough to participate in French. (+2 points)

Total contribution points today (out of 10)_____

With more advanced language learners, it is useful to support student reflection on class participation with a greater focus on improving speaking skills. A method developed and researched by Diane de Saint Leger (2009) involves the use of questionnaires that prompt students to reflect on their class participation and set goals for improvement periodically throughout the course. The questionnaire consists of brief multiple-choice or rating-scale questions that ask students to reflect on specific linguistic features. Depending on the objectives and proficiency level of the course, questions may focus on vocabulary, fluency, pronunciation, and turn taking, for example.

Students are then asked to set goals for improvement and identify the strategies they can use to achieve those goals. Providing the first questionnaire within the early weeks of the term helps students establish an awareness of areas they need to improve and set goals related to class participation and oral proficiency. Using follow-up questionnaires two additional times throughout the course, students are supported in developing important language learning habits for self-monitoring, assessing progress, and revising goals as needed. In de Saint Leger's research, students said that this self-assessment strategy helped to increase their awareness of ways to improve their speaking skills as well as their confidence in class participation.

Reflection

Think about the varied assessment strategies you use in your world language course.

- Are there predictable patterns of where students experience the greatest difficulty?
- What self-assessment strategies can you implement to help students monitor their performance and set goals for improvement?

SUMMARY

This chapter provided key strategies for reexamining and enhancing common assessment practices in world language classrooms. Beginning with a review of foundational concepts for planning inclusive assessments, discussion turned to strategies for identifying barriers in assessment practices and ways to increase the flexibility and choice provided for students. The important task of error correction was examined, and practical tips were provided for developing a more intentional plan for why, when, and how feedback is given. Finally, grading rubrics and self-assessment tools were explored for making the assessment process more explicit for students.

In chapter 5 a road map is provided to support you in pulling together an instructional plan that incorporates the many strategies provided in this book. Beginning with a challenge to explore your specific campus resources and student population, discussion turns to some final considerations in planning and connecting with your students in the important first three weeks of class.

Chapter 5

Getting Started

The preceding chapters have laid the ground work for becoming a more inclusive world language instructor. With an increased understanding of UDI we have made an intentional shift in thinking about students with disabilities. Anticipating diversity and the possible barriers students may experience raises awareness of the many ways you can make teaching more inclusive beginning with the design stage of your teaching.

Now that you have a variety of inclusive instructional strategies and assessment approaches in your teaching repertoire, some of the most important work still lies ahead. This chapter describes the essential task of connecting to your university, including tuning into the characteristics of your student population and using the resources and supports that are available on campus. We also provide several tools and prompts for continuing your growth as an inclusive world language instructor. It is time for a final step in applying the strategies you have been reading about in the preceding chapters.

CONNECTING TO YOUR CAMPUS

Who Are the Students on Your Campus?

In chapter 2 we talked about strategies for getting to know the students in your classroom. Using activities such as asking students about their prior learning and experiences with world languages prompts student metacognition while also helping the instructor get a sense of individual student needs. If you are new to the faculty or will be teaching on the same campus for more than one term, it is useful to step back and get a broader perspective of the student population as a whole. This will give you context for anticipating the needs of future students.

Campus demographic data, including typical student profiles, are often posted on the institution's Academic Affairs or institutional research website. Consider how these factors influence the design of your world language course:

- Are students primarily local or from out of state?
- What percentage of students finish a degree in two, four, or six years?
- What percentage of the population is made up of first-generation college students?
- Do students tend to come from metropolitan areas, where exposure to languages other than English might be expected, or from rural areas, where such exposure might be limited or highly contextualized?

Answers to these questions will help you modulate instruction to best serve students.

Another student demographic that is useful to know relates to the presence of students with disabilities:

- What percentage of students on campus register with the disability resource office?
- What are the most frequently disclosed types of disabilities?

This information may be posted on the disability resource office website. But if not, disability resource offices typically collect these data and are happy to share them with faculty. This information will help you anticipate the kinds of barriers students may encounter in your classroom and help you prioritize where to assure you have considered inclusive planning and teaching strategies.

Working with the Disability Resource Office

Most campuses have a disability resource office (also referred to as disability services or accessibility services on some campuses). These offices typically have one or more professionals on staff to answer your questions about working with students with disabilities. They are also the professionals who help the institution assure that it follows federal laws mandating nondiscrimination.

You may recall from the discussion in chapter 1 that in college, it is the student's responsibility to self-disclose if he or she has a disability and would like to request accommodations. Most often, this happens when students contact the disability resource office and follow the institution's procedures for registering with that office. This process typically entails providing documentation of the disability that is written by a qualified professional such as a psychologist, psychiatrist, educational diagnostician, or medical professional (e.g., an audiologist or ophthalmologist).

The disability resource office meets individually with each student to discuss the documentation and consider how the disability may impact the student in the college setting. This interview is the mechanism by which the disability resource professional determines which accommodations the student is eligible to receive on campus. You may recall from the case study of Janay in chapter 2 that accommodations and services that the student received in high school do not directly carry over to the college setting. They are determined based on the documentation provided and the new and more academically challenging context of college.

Students who have completed the process of registering with the institution's disability resource office will present you with a *faculty accommodation letter*, typically on office letterhead or e-mailed directly from the disability resource office. This letter specifies which accommodations the student may need in your class. If a student requests a disability-based accommodation but does not have a faculty accommodation letter, refer the student to the campus disability resource office. This step is essential for helping the institution assure consistency and compliance with federal law.

Sometimes the accommodations listed on the faculty accommodation letter do not appear to clearly apply to a world language class. For example, *priority seating* may be essential for a student needing to sit in the front of a large and crowded lecture hall. This accommodation becomes less relevant in a world language classroom with desks arranged in small clusters or pods. Other times you may wonder how to implement an accommodation in your class. A frequent accommodation, for instance, is extended test time. How does this accommodation work with the auditory and verbal components of world language assessments?

In these situations, feel free to reach out to the disability resource office to ask for clarification or suggestions. The accommodations that are listed on the faculty accommodation letter are often intended to apply to college classrooms, in general, without consideration of the specific instructional environment of the world language classroom. Disability resource office professionals often appreciate the chance to discuss possible student barriers and accommodation strategies with you to better fit the structure of your classroom.

Some additional accommodations typically used in world language classrooms include

- conducting the oral component of the test in the instructor's office,
- having dictation for tests repeated by the instructor or recorded for repeated listening,
- allowing the student to write dictated questions before composing responses, and
- permitting extended time to formulate replies on oral exams.

The work of disability resource offices is changing over time. While professionals in these roles offer support to individual students with disabilities, they also play an integral role in assuring access for individuals with disabilities across campus. On many campuses, for example, the disability resource website includes a feature that allows you to report a barrier on campus. Whether it is automatic door openers that aren't working or the frequently broken elevator experienced by Angie in our case study in chapter 2, every member of the campus community can contribute to campus awareness and resolution of barriers.

Disability resource offices are also embracing the much larger work of campus diversity initiatives. Partnerships with multicultural centers provide new opportunities for raising awareness of disability as an aspect of student diversity. The relatively new academic discipline of disability studies offers connections with the work of disability resource offices to consider a "culture" of disability. You may find that these ways to connect with the disability resource office lead to new perspectives on the students you teach.

Reflection

- What do you know about the general demographic characteristics of students on your campus? How does this influence your instruction?
- Do you feel prepared for responding to student requests for accommodations in your class? What additional questions do you have for your campus disability resource office?

DEVELOPING A PLAN FOR YOUR INSTRUCTION

Just as the work of disability resource offices changes over time, so the process of becoming an inclusive world language instructor is an ongoing endeavor. Each of the many instructional strategies discussed so far will enhance your classroom environment as you become more attuned to new aspects of student diversity. Putting these strategies together in a step-by-step plan is often useful in making sure good intentions to make changes in the classroom come to fruition. The following tools and prompts will help in this process. And when you are ready to continue your exploration of inclusive teaching, we share some strategies and experiences of other faculty who have continued to challenge themselves in this instructional domain.

Before Classes Begin

Now that you are aware of the general student population on your campus and attuned to the students you are likely to have in your classroom, it is time to review the basic elements of your course for a class infrastructure that is ready for diverse students. Remember that while this book approaches this topic from the perspective of anticipating students with disabilities, the proactive steps you incorporate at this design stage can be a lifeboat for many different learners, including

- those new to the challenges of college-level world language courses,
- those who may have been assigned individual education plans in high school that exempted them from world language courses,
- those who are hesitant to disclose a diagnosed disability,
- those undiagnosed students who have always wondered about their capacity to learn another language, or
- those who—fully aware of their learning needs and previous accommodations—merely need to know that the instructor, in a sense, "speaks the language of disabilities."

As part of your instructional review, it is important to anticipate the disability and academic supports your students may need. Now is the time to familiarize yourself with the services and resources available to students on your campus.

When a student—invited by the disability statement on your syllabus—approaches you to discuss accommodations or learning needs, do you know what to say? Anticipating the following questions will help you prepare for this conversation:

- Where is the disability resource office located?
- How does the student go about arranging accommodations for the class?
- What is the campus policy regarding modifications or course substitutions in world language courses?
- What other academic supports for language learning are available on campus?
- How can the student contact a tutor?

- How much independence do you have to grant unofficial modifications to the course?
- How would you respond to students without a diagnosed disability who confide that they have always struggled in world language classes?

After you find these answers from your world languages department and campus disability resource office, create a sheet detailing the information for easy future reference—or to share with your colleagues.

With these final details in place, it's time for a self-check. Textbox 5.1 provides a summary list of the planning and actions that we described in detail in chapter 2. Completing these tasks before classes begin will contribute to an inclusive world language classroom. How many of the inclusive features have you already achieved? What still remains on your list of preparations before classes begin?

TEXTBOX 5.1   SELF-CHECK: INCLUSIVE CLASSROOM FEATURES BEFORE CLASS BEGINS*

1. **The course syllabus**
   - ☐ Essential features, including major course components and instructor contact information, are clearly defined.
   - ☐ The document is easy to read and uses visual appealing elements such as tables and professional typefaces.
   - ☐ The document provides a balance of details and conciseness.
   - ☐ The document provides online links or directs students to additional information about future assignments and projects.
   - ☐ The document contains a disability statement.
   - ☐ The document is posted on the class website before the class begins.
2. **Instructional materials**
   - ☐ Textbook(s) and instructional materials are posted online at least four weeks before classes begin and include ISBN numbers.
   - ☐ Textbook(s) and instructional materials are available in multiple formats.
   - ☐ Selected videos have closed captioning, subtitles when appropriate, or a transcript.
3. **The physical layout of the room**
   - ☐ Desks are arranged to promote student-to-student and faculty-to-student interaction.

> - ☐ Lighting options are flexible for different instructional activities.
> - ☐ A plan is in place to modify room layout for group work, allowing for student communication and pathways for travel.
>
> **4. Dispositions that foster a positive classroom climate**
> - ☐ The instructor provides options for office hours, including face-to-face and virtual options.
> - ☐ The instructor is aware of disability resource office location and procedures.
> - ☐ The instructor is aware of other campus supports for students.
>
> *Source: Self-Check: Inclusive Classroom Features before Class Begins*, by Sally S. Scott and Wade A. Edwards. Farmville, VA: Longwood University. Copyright 2012. Reprinted with permission.
>
> * See chapter 2 for more details and suggestions related to each item in this checklist.

During the First Three Weeks

Once classes begin, your work as an inclusive world language instructor shifts from anticipating possible student diversity to connecting with and getting to know the individual students in your class. The first three weeks are an important time for building connections with students, clarifying expectations, and establishing a supportive classroom community. The following tips will help you prioritize and plan for a productive start-up to class.

Tip 1: Get to Know the Students in Your Class

The period before the first major assessment is an opportune time to get to know your students as individuals by planning activities that require students to talk about themselves. Not only do such activities personalize the target language and facilitate fluency, but they also make language meaningful, help introduce students to one other, and lower their affective filter.

Such engagement also conveys an important awareness that each student brings specific needs to the classroom. As Marshall Gregory (2008) notes, "The classroom world in which teachers think of themselves as primarily teaching *students* is a different classroom world from the one in which teachers think of themselves as primarily teaching *disciplines*" (p. 123, emphasis added). This is a vital distinction to make, particularly at the start of the term when inclusive classroom chemistry is developing.

When you participate fully in opening-day activities, divulging the same personal information asked of the students, you demonstrate a candidness that students find critical to learning.

As you get to know students, it is important to verify the correct placement of students in the world language course sequence. Placement procedures vary widely across campuses. Some institutions conduct an online exam to gauge a student's linguistic background and abilities; some assess students through individual oral interviews; others ask students to submit writing samples; still others rely on grades from high school transcripts.

In many institutions, the instructor is not involved in registering students for the course and must assume that the course is pitched at the appropriate level for those enrolled. Whatever method is used, whether a student learning autobiography, a placement test, an entrance interview, or some other diagnostic instrument, it is worthwhile during the first week of class to assure that each student has enrolled in a course commensurate with his or her abilities and experience. If a student with the abilities of a novice lands in an intermediate-level course, for instance, removing a barrier to learning is as simple as enrolling the student in a more suitable course.

Tip 2: Use the Target Language from the Very First Day

All students will come to the class wondering how they will fit in linguistically. In chapter 3 we talked about how common it is for students to find this performance aspect of world language learning to be stressful. This anxiety, hardly unique to students with disabilities, needs to be addressed as early as possible. When you expect students to engage in the target language from the very beginning of the course, you implicitly confront two questions that most students have in mind:

- How do I measure up to the other students in the class?
- How much of the target language can I expect to encounter?

A useful way to end the first day of class is to discuss these questions head-on. A 10-minute conversation about the importance of using the target language—including strategies for student improvement and assurances that fluency is not expected—will establish high expectations while demonstrating an awareness of student anxiety and concern.

The first three weeks of class are a prime time to incorporate some of the supports and strategies for target language described in chapter 3. Provide a list of useful classroom expressions in the target language. These lists are frequently included on the inside cover of course textbooks; you could display them prominently at the front of the classroom or make them into a bookmark.

Aside from the practical support of these lists, and the respect for the target language they instill, you can also use them to infuse a classroom with a genial personality. What should students say when someone sneezes? What should they say when they arrive late to class? How would students say "I brought you a delicious mocha grande" or "French is my favorite class"? This list could also be flexible and personalized, with new expressions added every week.

Tip 3: Make Classroom Structures Explicit

The time you spent in planning and developing your course syllabus and instructional materials before class began will now be put to good use. Provide the course syllabus on the first day of class and include time to highlight and discuss the major elements of the course. Show students the class website and where more specific details will be provided in future weeks of the course. Plan for periodic, built-in conversations about both the mechanics of the course and your expectations as instructor.

Walk students through the textbook design to show them how it is organized and how it will be used during the semester. Consider the following:

- Are some sections more vital than others?
- Is a vocabulary bank included at the end of each section, or are new words integrated contextually?
- Will the class encounter every reading passage and every cultural explanation, or will certain excerpts be highlighted?

During the first week of the term, a visually stimulating, highly detailed foreign-language textbook may be taxing to some students. Discussing and decoding the layout of the text can help students understand how to anticipate the rhythm of the course, how to pinpoint important topics, and how to connect the text with the syllabus and homework assignments.

For instance, "As noted in the syllabus, a vocabulary quiz will occur every Monday; the vital expressions are always found in the blue boxes on the first page of every chapter." Such an exercise in "textbook translation" helps ensure that essential information is perceptible to the student. Making useful learning structures explicit also helps students monitor their own preparation and learning.

Tip 4: Establish a Routine for Interactive Communication and Group Work

To foster a healthy classroom chemistry beginning with the first week of class, it is worthwhile to anticipate probable areas of student concern. Speaking a second language to a room of strangers always puts students in a vulnerable position. Not only are they asked to discuss sometimes personal aspects of their life, but they are asked to do so without the interpersonal and interpretive skills developed in their native language. When instructors purposefully design the way they group students or form teams, they establish inclusive routines.

Chance does play an outsized role in grouping students for language learning. As discussed in chapter 3, when the activity is a brief exchange, such as a warm-up exercise, students will most often collaborate with the person sitting next to them, whether that person is a friend they know outside of class or just the person who chose that seat randomly on the first day of the semester.

While the comfort of a familiar face can help lower an affective filter, the pairing of poorly matched neighbors can hinder learning if it is prolonged for weeks at a time. In the first weeks of class, observe these interactions to learn more about your students. Begin to use intentional strategies to configure communication partners in other ways: counting off by four, grouping students by birthdays or first names, and randomly distributing playing cards and grouping students by suits. Culturally relevant artifacts such as postcards or train schedules that tie into a lesson or theme can be substituted for playing cards. Using postcards or downloaded pictures, imagine creating a "cathedral" group and a "castle" group, or a "Monet" team and a "Picasso" team, that collaborates from time to time throughout the semester.

The objective here is to imitate realistic use of the language by giving students practice interacting with a wide variety of other students but without requiring them to negotiate their own introductions or form their own teams. Observing student interactions and mingling with the class during pair or group activities are prime opportunities to learn more about your students and gain insight into how you may need to further refine your grouping of students.

Pairing activities can be controlled to varying degrees by the instructor so that individual student needs can be accommodated discreetly. For example, a student with autism may display nontraditional social skills when working with peers. His speech may be loud, his prosody may be atypical, and he may sit too close to his partner. Discovering that this student works particularly well with one of his classmates, you may intentionally structure group work for this pair to work together consistently. Alternatively, if a consistent pairing is taxing to a student, the instructor should stay attuned to the need for using a class-wide strategy for rotating partners.

In observing group interaction, you may notice some students have difficulty with native language skills such as listening comprehension or attention to multistep directions. For example, if students break into teams and are given 10 minutes to develop a role play, does one of the teams get stuck just deciphering the directions? Use these diagnostic insights to enhance your instructions for group work. In addition to giving verbal instructions, provide directions for the teams in a visual format such as a PowerPoint slide as well. Contextualizing the activity before the class breaks into groups and modeling an ideal role play or verbal exchange would also support team performance and focus.

Tip 5: Manage Homework Expectations

Just as inclusive designers carefully consider the process of creating student groups and communication partners, they will be thoughtful about the work they ask students to prepare outside of class. There are many implicit understandings about homework that should be foregrounded at the beginning of the semester. Make time during the first week of class to talk with students about these points:

- How do the assigned exercises address the topics to be covered in class? Will students be expected to learn material independently, before a new concept is introduced in class? Or, does the assignment function more as a demonstration of knowledge already acquired?
- How do the assigned exercises help students review material that will not be addressed specifically in class?
- What expectations does the instructor have as the student is completing homework assignments? Is it expected that the student will consult the textbook? Should the student consult an online dictionary? Is it legitimate for students to work together to enlist the help of a tutor? How long should the student take to complete the assignment?
- When will homework be collected—and how does that schedule match the pedagogy of the instructor or the learning objectives of the class?
- To what degree does the format of homework exercises prepare students for the format of a unit test or other forms of high-stakes assessments?

By anticipating and answering these questions, instructors help students use homework effectively. During the early weeks of the semester, guide students through the process of homework completion so that they are aware of the best strategies for learning. Conversations about the homework will also reduce anxiety about what is unfamiliar and train students in acquiring habits that will help them be successful in other stages of language acquisition, as well as in other classes altogether.

In chapter 3, we discussed some of the barriers that arise when the homework is completed online and scored automatically. Instructors who use online assignments should prepare for an additional layer of concern:

- What should students do when they cannot understand the directions of a particular exercise?
- How will you address those inevitable situations when the student provides a valid answer that the program just doesn't recognize?

Responding to these questions before the students attempt homework exercises will stave off student frustrations that divert them from the linguistic or cultural lessons under consideration.

Tip 6: Respond to Early Quizzes and Grades

In the early weeks of class there are many opportunities for students to begin to receive feedback on their performance. Whether in the form of grades such as scores received on early vocabulary quizzes or homework assignments or more informal feedback such as error correction during class participation, the first three weeks are an important time to establish a learning environment that encourages student self-reflection and goal setting.

Include time in class to talk about error patterns on early quizzes. How did students study? Where did they experience difficulty? What strategies do they need to use in preparing for the first unit test? Prepare the first exam wrapper to be distributed to students with the completion of the test.

This is also the time to begin the process of student reflection on class participation. Whether a simple self-assessment to monitor good student habits such as speaking only the target language in class or a more refined self-assessment to establish goals for improving pronunciation or fluency, the tools and strategies described in chapter 4 should be implemented in the first three weeks to instill this metacognitive habit in classroom routines. Textbox 5.2 provides a checklist for reviewing these six tips.

TEXTBOX 5.2   DURING THE FIRST THREE WEEKS: USING INCLUSIVE STRATEGIES TO CONNECT WITH STUDENTS

1. **Start to get to know the students in your class.***
   - ☐ Use activities that require students to talk about themselves. Personalize the language and make it meaningful. Join in these conversations and share information about yourself.
   - ☐ Verify appropriate placement of all students. For placement issues, students should visit the language department chair or the language program coordinator.

2. **Use the target language from the very first day.***
   - ☐ Use an activity such as a scavenger hunt that requires the students also to speak in the target language.
   - ☐ Provide a list of useful classroom expressions to assist students with asking questions in the target language.
   - ☐ Talk about the challenges and reasonable expectations in learning to use the target language.
3. **Make classroom structures explicit.****
   - ☐ Walk students through the syllabus to highlight key features, class policies, and instructor availability.
   - ☐ Show students how to anticipate and plan for the rhythm of the course, such as weekly quizzes and homework. Show students where they can locate additional information about future assignments and projects.
   - ☐ Walk students through the textbook to show them how it is organized. Help students understand how to pinpoint important topics or learning features in the textbook.
4. **Begin to think about how you will group students in different ways for future activities.***
   - ☐ Observe student interactions during group work. Use intentional strategies to allow students to work with different communication partners.
   - ☐ Consider whether groups are functioning effectively. Provide explicit directions or modeling as needed.
   - ☐ Assign tasks and responsibilities within groups, rather than leaving this to chance.
5. **Discuss your expectations for learning and have students talk about their own experiences and expectations as a language learner. Work to create a welcoming environment for learning.****
   - ☐ Talk about your error correction strategies; let students know that errors are an expected part of the learning process.
   - ☐ Make students aware of other campus supports and services.
   - ☐ Be sure to be available during your posted office hours face-to-face as well as online.
6. **Respond to early quizzes and grades.*****
   - ☐ Provide class time to talk with students about errors on early quizzes and study strategies for future quizzes and tests.
   - ☐ Implement student self-assessment tools to encourage deeper processing of the language learning process.

> *Source*: *During the First Three Weeks: Using Inclusive Strategies to Connect with Students*, by Sally S. Scott and Wade A. Edwards. Farmville, VA: Longwood University. Copyright 2012. Reprinted with permission.
>
> * See chapter 3.
> ** See chapter 2.
> *** See chapter 4.

A Plan for Change over Time

In the process of implementing inclusive teaching strategies and becoming attuned to UDI as an approach to instructional design, some faculty find they want to know more. While the strategies and tips provided in this book are not onerous to implement, it does take practice and experience to achieve a fully welcoming and inclusive world language classroom. As you embrace this process, you may find you are ready for additional refinements to your class.

One approach many instructors find useful is to identify one or two aspects of the design of the course that you want to enhance each semester. You may identify these goals based on your own observations and reflection about interactions and student success in class. For example, after learning about the importance of flexibility in the UDI framework, and reading about options for student assessment in chapter 4, you might decide to take some time before the beginning of the next term and focus on student assessment processes in your class. How might you revise your tests or projects? Are there ways you can introduce more student choice?

Alternatively, you may find that student feedback or end-of-the-term course evaluations prompt your thinking about aspects of your class that could be enhanced. For example, how might you use this student comment to focus future course design? "The group work activities were really frustrating. No one knew what we were supposed to do. We wasted a lot of time."

However you choose to identify your instructional goals, it's important to remember that *every* world language class can *always* be made more inclusive. Inclusion is an interactive process of teaching, reflection, and enhancement. Once you are ready to continue to explore your inclusive teaching, the practice of selecting a targeted area for change over time makes this process manageable. For example, by targeting inclusive group work one semester, assessment practices the next term, and supplemental learning supports the following year, you can focus on the bigger picture of your teaching. For experienced teachers, choosing one aspect to focus on each term is a nice way to refresh instruction without redesigning an entire course.

Building Awareness and Skills in Designing Accessible Instructional Materials

In chapter 2 we provided some tips for making instructional materials more accessible before classes begin. For quick improvements we suggested two primary approaches: Provide material online to allow students the greatest flexibility for use and provide information about instructional materials such as textbooks or readings as early as possible. With sufficient advanced notice, the student or the campus disability resource office has time to convert the material into an accessible format.

When you are ready to build on this foundation, there are simple ways to make the use of your instructional materials more seamless. You can design your tests, quizzes, PowerPoint slides, and handouts, for example, to be more usable with the variety of technology and media used by your students.

A good starting place for improving the accessibility of your instructional materials is to investigate and take advantage of campus resources and training. As more and more colleges and universities recognize the importance of accessible electronic information technology, campus initiatives to promote awareness and skills are growing. These campus initiatives often involve a collaboration of departments across campus, including the disability resource office, the information technology office, and the teaching and learning center.

Look at their websites for useful links or upcoming training events. Attend a workshop on how to create accessible Word, PowerPoint, and PDF files. Visit your teaching and learning center on campus and ask about consultation on accessibility. Talk with your colleagues in the disability resource office about how your instructional materials could be more accessible.

Another option is to take advantage of online resources and public training modules. ACTFL and statewide foreign-language associations will schedule occasional webinars, many of which offer recertification points. If you prefer to work on your own, or perhaps plan to develop skills over the summer during some time away from campus, the website of WebAIM (Web Accessibility In Mind) is an excellent resource. See https://webaim.org/. Online materials include short articles on developing PowerPoint slides, PDF documents, and Word documents in accessible formats; designing instructional materials that are usable by individuals with color blindness; and experiencing what it's like to use a screen reader.

SUMMARY

This chapter has underscored two key elements in designing inclusive instruction: proactive awareness of student learning needs and systematic reflection of how to improve from semester to semester. To best engage students, you will ask them about themselves, understand the demographics of the classroom, connect with faculty colleagues and student affairs professionals—particularly the staff in the disability resources office—and consider methods for making materials fully accessible to diverse learners.

Recognizing that the first three weeks are crucial for establishing an inclusive rapport and routine, this chapter offers several tips to follow early in the semester and provides checklists to review at the outset of the semester. Finally, this chapter reminds you to be deliberate and purposeful in your instruction and planning. Inclusive teaching is attentive teaching that changes constantly in response to the individuals in your class.

Chapter 6 offers some concluding thoughts about UDI and world language learning. Responses to some frequently asked questions are provided, and ideas are offered for how you might share your new perspectives on inclusive teaching with colleagues across campus.

Chapter 6

Conclusions

Universal Design for Instruction (UDI) provides a lofty goal for teaching: to design and deliver instruction in a manner that maximizes learning opportunities for all students. With a particular focus on students with disabilities, this book has described strategies for becoming more attuned to student diversity and established some fundamental steps of inclusive instructional design.

We began with a discussion of the world language course infrastructure grounded with an inclusive syllabus, accessible instructional materials, and a welcoming instructor mind-set. Next, we explored teaching strategies and methods, including ways to rethink some of the essential tools of world language classrooms such as use of target language, group activities, and homework. We looked closely at assessment of student learning and how to expand or reframe our approaches. And as a final step in the process, we have discussed ways to connect with your campus and the specific students in your classroom.

The strategies presented in this book are not an exhaustive list of UDI teaching methods, but they do start you on the path of inclusive course design. In our experiences over the course of a decade of work on the topic of disability and world language learning, we continue to learn through our ongoing collaboration and conversations with colleagues. The many barriers and student scenarios that have been shared, discussed, and researched continue to challenge our thinking and approaches to instructional design.

In these closing thoughts, we present some remaining questions that we often encounter in our workshops. We also share some of our experience expanding the work of inclusive world language learning from a focus on individual classrooms to a departmental collaboration that promotes inclusive teaching more broadly. We encourage you to start to think about ways you can share what you have learned about inclusive instruction in this book with colleagues on your campus.

FREQUENTLY ASKED QUESTIONS

Q: How much support is appropriate when working with a student with a disability or assisting students who struggle?

A: The answer to this question will depend on the student and the circumstance. At a minimum, university instructors are required by law to make the appropriate accommodations that are determined by the campus disability resource office. See chapter 5 for information on typical campus procedures in this area, including how you can contact the disability resource office to discuss questions or concerns with recommended accommodations.

Beyond these required accommodations, however, faculty members are encouraged to think about the broader issues of inclusive course design. Talk with students about barriers they are experiencing. Use the UDI principles to generate strategies that may assist many students in the classroom. Don't forget to let students know about other support services that can help.

Q: Once an instructor incorporates inclusive teaching and assessment strategies, will this eliminate the need for accommodations for individual students?

A: The goal of using inclusive teaching practices and eliminating classroom barriers is certainly to make the world language classroom more usable and effective for a wide variety of students. In fact, research is emerging that supports the finding that inclusive teaching does reduce the need for many of the most common classroom accommodations.

However, even very good course design may not anticipate every barrier experienced by students. If a student with a disability still needs accommodations and has followed the institution's procedures for making a request, the instructor should comply with institutional practices and provide the accommodation. As always, if you have questions or concerns about the accommodation, it is appropriate to discuss this with the campus disability resource office.

Q: How do you approach a student who needs assistance but hasn't disclosed a disability?

A: Sometimes instructors observe discrepancies in a student's performance such as strong participation in class but extremely low performance on written tests or perhaps a student who appears to be working diligently but is not learning the material. At the college level, students have the option to disclose a disability or not, making this discrepancy in performance sometimes hard to understand. Does the student have a disability that he or she chooses not to reveal to the faculty member? Does the student possibly have a disability that has not been previously diagnosed? What should an instructor do in this type of situation?

If you are concerned about a student's performance in your class, it is appropriate to ask to speak to the student in a private setting, such as during your office hours. Since you don't know the source of the student's difficulties, we recommend that you focus on the behavior that you have observed. Talk with the student about how he or she learns best and what has worked in the past to support learning.

In the course of this conversation, the student may disclose a disability. He or she may also mention an IEP or a 504 Plan that was used in high school. These two documents are individualized plans that are provided in K-12 education to accommodate students with disabilities. If these topics arise, the student should be referred to the campus disability resource office so the student can learn about how this process works at the college level.

If the student does not mention a diagnosed disability, refer the student to a variety of campus resources such as tutoring services, language labs, and academic support. You can suggest that the student may wish to also follow up with the disability resource office to talk with a staff member about what the student is experiencing and possible next steps.

Q: Is there a foreign-language learning disability?

A: Over the years, this question has been a hot topic of debate. Most recently, however, scholars have published case studies and other research-based evidence that there is no learning disability connected solely to learning a second language. When students have a disability that has a significant impact in their native language, such as difficulty with phonological processing needed for decoding words or spelling, it is very likely they will also experience similar difficulty in the second language.

Consider some of the common learning demands of language acquisition: memorization of new vocabulary and grammatical structures, writing and spelling skills, recognizable speech, social communication, and peer interaction. Few disciplines require student learning outcomes across the broad scope of aural, oral, reading, and written dimensions. Language learning is also a cumulative process requiring self-discipline for practice to reach fluency and automaticity. The process of acquiring a language draws on multiple areas of learning that, when combined, can create unique challenges.

You may be wondering, *Isn't this the same thing as a foreign-language learning disability?* This type of disability profile can affect students in very different ways. Some students may have had extensive early academic support and have now developed sufficient compensation strategies. World language learning will still be challenging, but possible.

The effectiveness of instruction and the level of support available on campus are also big factors in the success of these students in the world language classroom.

Q: When is a foreign-language waiver or course substitution considered an appropriate accommodation?

A: Waivers or course substitutions for a campus foreign-language requirement are a matter of institutional policy. Most colleges and universities with a foreign-language requirement have a procedure in place for considering this accommodation. The accommodation request and review process typically involve input from the campus disability resource professional, world language faculty, and administrators or committees charged with reviewing student requests for exceptions to general education requirements.

Q: I sometimes view the work of a student and wonder, "How did she get into college?" Does a disability mean there are intellectual deficits present?

A: No. There is no special admissions process for students with disabilities. They submit college applications and are reviewed and considered for admission under the same criteria as any other student on your campus. In fact, colleges are not allowed to ask students about the presence of a disability as part of the college application process to help assure that these applicants are reviewed using the same standards as any other student.

An exception to this rule may occur if your college has a program specifically designed for students with disabilities. These specialized programs are not the same entity as the campus disability resource office. They typically have their own application and admission process and may charge additional fees for student enrollment.

Q: Are students required to register with the campus disability resource office?

A: No. At the college level, students have the option to decide whether they choose to disclose a disability or not. If the student chooses not to register with the disability resource office, however, he or she is not eligible to receive accommodations on campus.

The Office of Disability Resources encourages students to register with the office early in their educational careers to assess learning barriers. Early contact with students with language-based disabilities facilitates discussions concerning the need for additional accommodations specific to world language learning, course substitutions, and/or course waivers when appropriate. Registering with the disability resource office allows administrators and foreign-language instructors to proactively assess and monitor the student's progress in world language courses.

WORKING WITH COLLEAGUES ON CAMPUS

In our work with world language faculty over the years, we have received regular feedback from workshop participants and colleagues. The tools and strategies provided in this book increase instructor comfort levels and a sense of self-efficacy for working with students with disabilities. Research with faculty from a variety of academic disciplines has shown that understanding campus resources and using a UDI framework for addressing student barriers have many positive outcomes for students as well. While research is still in early stages, some emerging findings include a greater sense of student self-determination, reduced need for retrofitted accommodations, and increased persistence in coursework.

Under a grant from the U.S. Department of Education, the authors worked with a team of world language instructors to examine the applications of UDI and gather data on student outcomes (Edwards & Scott, 2012). At the outset of the project, students with disabilities and students without disclosed disabilities demonstrated differences in final grades. Over a four-year period, the average grade distribution of students with disabilities showed proportionately fewer final grades of As, Bs, or Cs in beginning and intermediate language courses. These students were also withdrawing from classes at a much higher rate than peers without disclosed disabilities.

To address these disparate outcomes, instructors identified where their students were experiencing difficulty in their classes and received training on the topics included in this book. Working as a learning community, the group met monthly for two semesters to share lunch and discuss the student barriers and inclusive strategies.

After completing this cycle of intensive learning community work for two cohorts of participants over a two-year period, the final grades of all students were reexamined. The final grades in beginning and intermediate language courses were now aligned for students with and without disabilities; an equal percentage of students were achieving As, Bs, or Cs. And, although students with disabilities were still slightly more likely to withdraw from a language course, these percentages were much closer to the general student population (Scott & Edwards, 2012).

These data-based student outcomes were achieved by collaborating with colleagues across the department to consider the barriers faced by students with disabilities and examine inclusive teaching practices. Are there ways you might be able to work with colleagues on your campus? We encourage you to continue your exploration of UDI and join or develop a cadre of peers to support your work. Using the case studies provided throughout this book is a great way to begin the process of discussing instructional dilemmas and inclusive teaching.

You may even find that your institution is willing to offer some support or incentives to encourage the work of enhancing teaching. Here are some incentives that may be available to you:

- Campus-based incentive grants to explore innovation in teaching
- Stipends for new technology in support of teaching
- Memberships to the ACTFL or the Modern Language Association (MLA)
- Recognition or honors for excellence in teaching that are viewed favorably in the promotion, tenure, and review process

Despite busy schedules, many instructors find that the time they commit to working with colleagues on the topic of inclusive teaching is time well spent. Gathering a learning community or affiliate group of likeminded colleagues can strengthen ties with peers on campus as well as expand insights about the students you all teach. Talking about teaching is a good way to recharge and reinvigorate your instruction. It also encourages your ongoing commitment to providing instruction that meets the learning needs of today's students that predictably include a range of students with disabilities.

SUMMARY

This chapter has focused on providing final resources and suggestions for your work to design and deliver an inclusive learning environment for students with disabilities and other diverse learners. Some remaining frequent questions were posed, and responses were provided. Strategies to continue your exploration of inclusive world language were offered.

It is hoped that the end of this book marks the beginning of a renewed sense of commitment to well-designed, inclusive world language instruction. As the authors discovered very early in their professional collaboration, the student-centered focus of the principles of Universal Design for Instruction and the pedagogy and objectives familiar to language instructors share a common purpose, namely the development of a culture in which all individuals, regardless of ability or language, are welcomed, understood, and included.

The ACTFL, in its position statement on global competence, affirms that the ability to communicate with respect and cultural understanding in more than one language is an essential element of modern education. While language instructors understand that their primary role is to assist students in acquiring respect and understanding for those outside their native culture, this book's emphasis on empathetic pedagogical design will help readers consider whether they are also developing that same respect and understanding for students who are a part of the native culture.

Empathy, as Sonia Cardenas (2018) has recently asserted, is an obvious by-product of design thinking and has always been integral to a humanistic education. Because design thinking challenges instructors to rethink how they engage students in the classroom, consistently putting their needs at the center of instruction, it overlaps and enhances the fundamental intentions of language educators. By bringing the design principles of UDI to bear on the teaching of world languages, you will put into practice—and train your students to put into practice—the vital empathetic ethos needed to be proficient communicators in a second language.

References

Ambrose, S., Bridges, M., DiPietro, M., Lovett, M., & Norman, M. (2010). *How learning works: Seven research-based principles for smart teaching*. San Francisco, CA: Jossey-Bass.

American Council on the Teaching of Foreign Languages. (2014). *World-Readiness Standards for Learning Languages*. Retrieved from https://www.actfl.org/publications/all/world-readiness-standards-learning-languages/standards-summary

Americans with Disabilities Act of 1990, Public Law 101-336 (1990).

Brown, A. (2009). Students' and teachers' perceptions of effective foreign language teaching: A comparison of ideals. *Modern Language Journal, 93*(1), 46–60.

Cardenas, S. (2018, May 29). What higher ed can learn from design thinking [Letter to the editor]. *Chronicle of Higher Education*. Retrieved from https://www.chronicle.com

Centers for Disease Control. (n.d.). *Autism spectrum disorder: Data and statistics*. Retrieved from https://www.cdc.gov/ncbddd/autism/data.html

de Saint Leger, D. (2009). Self-assessment of speaking skills and participation in a foreign language class. *Foreign Language Annals, 42*(1), 158–178.

Edwards, W., & Scott, S. (2012). Addressing the needs of contingent faculty and students with disabilities. *NECTFL Review, 70,* 15–30.

Gaston, P., Clark, J., Ferren, A., Maki, P., Rhodes, T., Schilling, K., & Smith, D. (2010). *General education & liberal learning: Principles of effective practice*. Washington, DC: Association of American Colleges & Universities.

Gregory, M. (2008). Do we teach disciplines or do we teach students? What difference does it make? *Profession,* 117–129.

Hainline, L., Gaines, M., Long Feather, C., Padilla, E., & Terry, E. (2010). Changing students, faculty, and institutions in the twenty-first century. *Peer Review, 12*(3), 12–24.

Hildebrandt, S. (2010, January). *Inclusive assessment*. Paper presented at Project LINC Topical Workshop, Longwood University.

Individuals with Disabilities Education Act, 20 U.S.C. Section 1400 (2004).

Krupnick, M. (2014, February 13). Colleges respond to growing ranks of learning disabled. *The Hechinger Report*. Retrieved from https://hechingerreport.org

Lovett, M. C. (2013). Make exams worth more than the grade: Using exam wrappers to promote metacognition. In M. Kaplan, N. Silver, D. Lavaque-Manty, & D. Meizlish (Eds.), *Using reflection and metacognition to improve student learning* (pp. 18–52). Sterling, VA: Stylus Publishing.

National Council of State Supervisors for Languages and American Council on the Teaching of Foreign Languages. (2017). *Can-Do statements*. Retrieved from https://www.actfl.org/publications/guidelines-and-manuals/ncssfl-actfl-can-do-statements

Scott, S., & Edwards, W. (2012). Project LINC: Supporting lecturers and adjunct instructors in foreign language classrooms. *Journal of Postsecondary Education and Disability, 25*(3), 253–258.

Scott, S., Hildebrandt, S., & Edwards, W. (2010). *Foreign Language Learning as Perceived by College Students with Disabilities: Barriers to Learning and Positive Experiences*. (Tech. Rep. No. 01). Project LINC. Farmville, VA: Longwood University.

Scott, S., Hildebrandt, S., & Edwards, W. (2013). Second language learning as perceived by students with disabilities. In B. Lado & C. Sanz (Eds.), *Issues in language program direction: Individual differences, L2 development & language program administration: From theory to application* (pp. 171–191). American Association of University Supervisors and Coordinators (AAUSC), Boston, MA: Cengage.

Simon, C. (2000). Dyslexia and learning a foreign language: A personal experience. *Annals of Dyslexia, 50,* 155–187.

Skomsvold, P. (2014, October). *Web tables: Profile of undergraduate students: 2011–2012 (NCES 2015–167)*. U.S. Department of Education. Washington, DC: National Center for Education Statistics. Retrieved from https://nces.ed.gov/pubs2015/2015167.pdf

Thurlow, M., Johnstone, C., & Ketterlin-Geller, L. (2008). Universal design of assessment. In S. Burgstahler & R. Cory (Eds.), *Universal design in higher education: From principles to practice* (pp. 73–81). Cambridge, MA: Harvard Education Press.

University of Vermont Student Accessibility Services. (2010, March 10). *An educational journey*. Retrieved from https://blog.uvm.edu/udl/2010/03/15/an-educational-journey-for-students-with-disabilities/

Vyatkina, N. (2010). The effectiveness of written corrective feedback in teaching beginning German. *Foreign Language Annals, 43*(4), 671–689.

Williams, J. (2014, September 22). College of tomorrow: The changing demographics of the student body. *US News & World Report*. Retrieved from https://www.usnews.com

Womack, A. (2018). *Accessible syllabus: Accessible classroom resources promote student engagement and agency*. Retrieved from https://accessiblesyllabus.tulane.edu/about-us/

Index

Page references for figures are italicized.

ACTFL. *See* American Council on the Teaching of Foreign Languages
academic accommodations, 5, 7–8, 11, 22, 27, 29, 34, 36–37, 41–43, 51–52, 54, 71–72, 79–80, 86, 93–95, 108, 110–11
academic supports, xii–xiii, xv, xviii, 5–7, *13–14*, 16, 21, 24, 26–27, 29, 34, 36, 42, 46–51, 53, 56, 66–67, 69, 71, 76–77, 79–81, 86–89, 91, 94–95, 97–99, 101, 103–4, 108–10, 112, 116–17
accessibility services. *See* disability resource office
accessible format, 28, 74, 81, 105. *See also* alternate format
access skills, 70, 73–74
adjunct instructors, 29, 116–17
admissions, 110
affective filter, 97, 100
alternate format, 27, 61, 70. *See also* accessible format
American Council on the Teaching of Foreign Languages (ACTFL), 8–9, 48, 54, 110, 112–13, 116
Americans with Disabilities Act (ADA), 4, 115

anxiety, 22, 29, 37–39, 41, 47–50, 52, 55, 68–69, 75–78, 81, 84, 98, 101
artifacts, 26, 46, 100
assessment, 12, 19, 68–75, 77, 79, 81, 83–89, 93, 97, 101–4, 107–8; formative, 67, 69, 77, 83–84, 87; summative, 69, 77, 83–84
assistive technology, 15–16, 27, 57
attention deficit hyperactivity disorder (ADHD), 4, 16–17, 28, 32–33, 35–36
aural components, 53–54, 109
autism spectrum, xii, 5, 10, 15, 17, 65–66, 100, 115
automated grading system, *64*, 67

barriers to learning, xii–xiii, xvi–xvii, 9–10, 12, 15–18, 20–22, 24–25, 28, 32, 34–35, 37, 39–42, 45, 47, 52, 54–55, 58–63, 66–70, 72–77, 81, 89, 92, 94, 101, 107–8, 110–11

Can-Do statements, 54–55
chronic health, xii, 4, 15
circumlocution, 16, 49, 82
class participation, 15, 24–25, *31*, 39, *48*, 56, 60, 71, 76, 80, 88–89, 102, 108

classroom community, *14*–15, 17, 20, 23, 25, 60, 72, 79–80, 94, *97*, 111–12
classroom layout, 19–20, 25, 31–32, 71, *96*–*97*, 99
classroom phrases, *49*, 53
closed captioning, 27, 96
communication partners, 55, 56, 58, 100–101
communicative classroom, 52, 57, 75
course substitutions, xii–xiii, 95, 110–11

demographics, 2
dictionary, 82, 101
disability, xi–xiii, 1, 3–12, 15, 18, 22, 24–25, 27, 29–30, 34–35, 37, 40–43, 51–52, 54, 56, 71–72, 77, 79, 86, 92–97, 107–11
disability resource office, xi, 25, 27, 29, 33–35, 40–43, 51, 54, 57, 64, 79–80, 86, 92–*97*, 105–6, 108–11
disability statement, 29–30, 32, 34, 80, 95–*96*
disability studies, 94
diversity, xiii, xvii, 1–5, 7–12, 18–19, 21, 24, 45, 75, 91, 94–95, 97, 107
documentation, 29, 93
dyslexia, xii, 84–86

economic status, 3
empathy, 113
equity, 42, 85–86
error correction, xvii, 39, 75–80, 89, 102–3
exam wrapper, 87, 102
executive functioning, 35, 62, 66, 87
extended test time, xi, *13*, 29, 41–43, 51, 79, 93–94

faculty accommodations letter, xi, 7, 36, 40–43, 51, 79, 93
federal laws, xi, 4, 92
Federal Education Rights and Privacy Act (FERPA), 7
504 plan, 32–33, 109

foreign-language learning disability, xi, 109–10
foreign language requirements, 20, 110
foreign language waiver, xi–xiii, 110–11. *See also* course substitutions

games, 17, 46, 48, 61
gender composition, 2
global competence, 113
grade contracts, 72
grading rubrics, xviii, 16, 28, 72, 77, 81, 83–84, 89
graduate teaching assistants, xviii, 29, 80
group activities, xviii, 9, 12–15, 17, 25, 46, 55–58, 60–61, 88, *97*, 100, *103*–4, 107
group formation, 56, 60, *103*
group grades, 30, 56–57, *103*

hearing impairment, 4, 21–22, 80
high school, xi–xii, xvii, 5, 20, 29, 34, 39, 42, 51–53, 65, 86, 93, 95, 98, 109
homework, xviii, *6*, 26, *31*, 33–36, 45, 50, 61–68, 74, 77, *83*–84, 87–*88*, 99, 101–3, 107; online, *12*, 15–16, 26, *31*, 33, 46, 63–67, *83*, 101, *103*, 105
humor, 46, 53

impairment, 4, 8, 10, 15–16, 21–22, 30, 57, 80
incentives, 112
inclusive routines, 64, 66, 100, 102
Individualized Education Program (IEP), xi, 6–7, 109
Individuals with Disabilities Education Act (IDEA), 5–6
information technology office, 105
instructional goals, *14*, 82, 87–89, 102, 104
instructional materials, 5, *6*, 8, *13*, 15–16, 19, 26–28, 43, 45–47, 50, 54, 64, 70–71, *96*, 99, 105–7

Index

instructor disposition, 19, 28, 36–39, 41, 43, 55, 76, 79, 97
interpersonal communication, 54–55, 100
interpretive communication, 54–55, 100
intersectionality, 5
ISBN, 27, *96*

learning disabilities (LD), xi–xiii, xvii–xviii, 4–11, 15–18, 20, 22, 28–29, 35–37, 42, 45–47, 64, 66, 68, 70, 76–77, 85–87, 91, 95, 98, 109–12
learning memory strategies, xii, 35, 46, 54, 64, 70
learning objectives, 26, 69–70, 72, 101, 112
learning outcomes, 9, 26, 69–70, 83, 85, 109, 111
learning pace, 12, *13*, 60
learning profile, xii, 15, 75, 85, 92, 110
lighting, 21, *97*

major life activity, 4
medical model of disability, 8, 24, 41
mental health, 4, 7
metacognition, xviii, 38, 49, 82, 86–87
minority populations, 2–3
multicultural center, 94
multimedia, 46
multimodal teaching, 46–47

non-apparent disabilities, 4, 22
nondiscrimination, 92
notetaking support, 27, 29, 51

Office of Civil Rights (OCR), 43
oral interviews, *31*, 48, 54, 76, 81–83, 89, 94, 98, 109

pairing activities, 56, 100
peer editing, 77
physical environment, 11, 17, 19–22, 24–25, 28, 43
phonological processing, 109

placement procedures, 98, *102*
presentational communication, 54–55
Principles of Universal Design for Instruction (UDI), xvii, 1, 11–15, 17–18, 22, 24, 26–29, 32, 34, 41, 47, 52, 60, 66, 74, 77, 80–81, 108, 112–13; community of learners, *14*, 15, 17, 20, 23, 25, 60, 79–80, 97, 111–12; equitable use, *13*, 15, 24, 60, 86; flexibility in use, *13*–15, 26, 47, 61, 66, 71–72, 86, 89, 104–5; instructional climate, 11, *14*, 17, 25, 32, 39, 41, 49, 52–53, 67, 78–*79*; low physical effort, *13*, 17; perceptible information, 4, *13*, 16, 26, 60, 81, 99; simple and intuitive, *13*, 16, 35, 50, 66; size and space for approach and use, *14*, 17, 20, 24; tolerance for error, *13*–14, 16–17, 34, 47, 52–53, 66, 84
proficiency, xv, 9–10, 49, 54, 75, 85, 88–89
projects, 15, 17, 28, 46, 56–57, 71–72, 87, *96*, *103*–4
psychological, 22, 56

quiz, *13*, 16, 27, *31*, 33, 40, 50–51, 57–58, 70–73, *83*, 99, 102–*3*, 105

reading materials, xii, 4, 16, 21, 27–28, 50, 61–62, 74, 99, 105, 109
repetition, 16, 46–47, 49, 53

screen reader, 27, 64, 105
self-advocacy, *6*, 30, 37
self-assessment, xviii, 69, 81, 86, 88–89, 102, *103*
self-determination, 68, 71, 111
self-disclosure, 4–5, 7, 34, 37, 79–80, 92, 95, 109–11
sensory disabilities, 4, *13*, 16
social interaction, 1, 15, 22, 55, 60, 100
social model of disability, xiii, 8, 12, 18

social skills, 55, 76, 100, 109
societal changes, 4
special education services, 4–5, 7, 42
student choice, *13*, 15–16, 26, 43, 72, 83, 89, 104
student identity, 4, 74
students who are blind, 4, 11, 26, 61, 105
students who are hard of hearing, 4, 17, 21, 80
students with disabilities, xi–xiii, xvi–xviii, 1, 3–11, 15–18, 20, 22, 28–29, 35–37, 42, 45–47, 64, 66, 68, 70, 76–77, 85–87, 91–92, 94–95, 98, 107, 109–12
syllabus, *6*, *13*, 15, 17, 19, 23–24, 27–36, 43, 62, 66, 80–81, 83, 95–*96*, 99, *103*, 107

target language, xii, xviii, 9, *13–14*, 20–21, 36, 43, 45–50, 52–53, 55–56, 62, 68, 71, 74, 81, 97–99, 102–*3,* 107
target skills, 69–70, 72–74, 79
teaching and learning center, xviii, 72, 105

textbooks, 1, 11, 16, 26–27, 30, 50, 53, 57, 74, 99, *103*, 105
transcripts, 98
transition to college, 5, 29, 34

undiagnosed students, 95
universal design (UD), 11, 19, 24, 58
Universal Design for Instruction (UDI), xiii, xvii–xviii, 1, 12, *13*–15, 17–18, 22, 24–27, 32, 34–35, 41–43, 47, 52, 59–60, 66, 71, 73–74, 79–81, 85–86, 91, 104, 106–8, 111–13

verbal communication, 16, 51, 76, 79–81, 101
visual impairment, 10, 16, 21, 30
visuals, 26, 46–47
vocabulary, 16, 46, 50, 53, 58, 60, 62, *82–83*, 86–88, 99, 102, 109

wheelchair users, 4, 11, 17, 22–24
working memory, 35, 54, 70
World-Readiness Standards for Language Learning, 1, 9–10
writing samples, 98

About the Authors

Sally S. Scott, PhD, is senior research associate for the Association on Higher Education and Disability (AHEAD), the premier professional association promoting equity and inclusion for college students with disabilities. She holds a doctorate from the University of Virginia and has more than 25 years' experience working with adolescents and young adults with a wide range of disabilities. Dr. Scott is the former editor of the *Journal on Postsecondary Education and Disability*. She has published and presented nationally and internationally on issues related to inclusive teaching, college support services, and emerging disability populations. She has authored and coauthored federal grants totaling more than $3 million and including three demonstration projects focusing on UDI. Along with coauthor, Wade A. Edwards, she directed Project LINC to develop training curricula to support adjunct and contingent world language faculty. Dr. Scott serves as senior research associate for the National Center on College Students with Disabilities and is a consultant to the Educational Testing Service.

Wade A. Edwards, a former department chair and modern languages program coordinator, is professor of French and associate dean of the Cook-Cole College of Arts & Sciences at Longwood University in Virginia. He is the recipient of the Maria Bristow Starke Award—Longwood's preeminent faculty honor—and the Inclusive Excellence Award for his work with diverse learners. His scholarship has appeared in *Nineteenth-Century French Studies*, *Feminist Teacher*, and the *NECTFL Review*, among other publications. A frequent presenter at national and international conferences, Dr. Edwards served as co-principal investigator with Sally S. Scott for the federally funded Project LINC and has been teaching French to college students at a variety of public universities for 25 years.

www.ingramcontent.com/pod-product-compliance
Lightning Source LLC
Chambersburg PA
CBHW021846220426
43663CB00005B/424